Successful
Selling

Successful Selling

Gerard I. Nierenberg

Made E-Z

PENTAGON PRESS
NEW DELHI

SUCCESSFUL SELLING

ISBN - 81-8274-957-3

First published in India in 2005 by

PENTAGON PRESS
A-38, Hauz Khas, New Delhi-110016 (India)
Phones: 011-51656996/7/8 • Tele-fax: 011-51656997
E-mail: pentagonpress@touchtelindia.net
www.pentagon-press.com

Printed by Elegant Printers, New Delhi.

Authorized reprint edition for sale in India, Pakistan, Bangladesh, Nepal & Sri Lanka.

Table of Contents

Table of Contents

Introduction

We all sell. We all buy. We all negotiate. Too often we think we are "born" salespeople or "born" negotiators, that childhood tricks of the trade will suffice for a lifetime. Some feel that selling is crass, while negotiation is a win-or-lose game they hope to win. Even more believe that if you wear two hats, you must have two heads. A few, the Supreme Court of California among them, believe that all occupations are pretty much alike. The court ruled in 1985 that Madame Fatima Stevens, a Gypsy fortune-teller and minister of the Spiritual Psychic Science Church of Truth of Azusa, was no different from an economist. Both professions involve "the passing of ideas and information-some valid, some questionable, some false."

Traditional past concepts of selling, buying, and negotiation can now join Madame Fatima and economists on the bench. All professional predictions of the future quickly become obsolete. The future becomes the present, then the past. This is so of sales and negotiation also, Unless they are viewed as processes rather than discrete events, that is, win-or-lose games. In a process world past, present, and future have equal weight. The only valid prediction that can be made is that things will change.

This book's primary purpose is not to provide you with "sure-fire tips on selling and buying." By their nature these tips impose limits on your creative thinking. Instead, it presents sales negotiation as a process with many surprising twists and turns that eventually may lead not to the division of an ever-shrinking pie (that would mean the process had ended and, in reality, processes have a certain immortality—but to the production of more pie—a pie big enough for everybody.

This book is designed to show how you, in selling and buying, can survive and succeed in an ever-changing process world. With it you can learn to make change an ally, not an enemy. Instead of attempting to manipulate buyers and sellers, you will learn how to negotiate with them to produce a cooperative solution where everyone wins. That's right—not just you or the buyer or the seller or society as a whole. Everybody! You'll be good in every transaction and good for something. You will close that big sale, and the profits will not be bad, either.

Gerard I. Nierenberg

Becoming a Master Negotiator

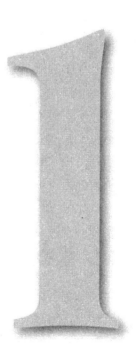

Becoming a Master Negotiator

"Everyone lives by selling something."

R. L. Stevenson Beggars

In a broad sense, all negotiations occur in the context of getting (or buying) and giving (or selling). You can consider selling and buying as only opposite sides of the same coin. All guidance that I offer for sales and master sales negotiators applies to the other side, the purchaser and the buyer, as well. Consider how it can apply to all transactions in which you are involved.

Sales negotiation shares several characteristics with other art forms:

- no one is born an artist
- an inherent talent may decide the direction a person takes, but mastery of the subject can come only after sufficient training and practice
- during these stages the practitioner will rise through various levels before he or she reaches mastery

Adam, Ben, and Carol operate competing businesses. Each has different sales-negotiating skills. Adam works very hard at persuading, convincing, and motivating customers. Ben works just as hard at offering things that satisfy ordinary needs. Carol develops an understanding of customers' problems and offers solutions. With whom would you rather deal?

11

Each of these three salespeople has developed varying degrees of skill at negotiating. Adam is a novice. Ben is a competent salesperson. Carol is a master sales negotiator. How do they differ? The Art of Negotiating® has at least three levels:

1) The novice negotiator

2) The competent negotiator

3) The master negotiator

Every human being starts from birth as a novice negotiator. No matter what our life preferences, we are compelled to negotiate for them. It is as inevitable as the sucking instinct with which we are born. However, at some period in development, many people make a conscious attempt to deal with negotiation thoughtfully. As novices they learn the vocabulary of negotiating and attempt to understand its subject matter. They may even make stilted attempts at changing their negotiating appearance and mannerisms to create a more "appropriate" image.

The result? In all too many cases, in negotiations with more experienced people, novices have a long, hard time concluding the negotiation. They may be subjected to unfair, even drastic, demands or to barely concealed hostility or contempt. This is because the more experienced negotiator feels, fairly or not, that the novices are at best, inexperienced, and at worst, stupid. One common reason is that novices think that having mastered the vocabulary and some knowledge of, for example, real estate, they are ready to negotiate a real estate deal. Not so. Two totally different vocabularies and information systems are involved in negotiating and in real estate. Constructive communication between opposing sides in the deal and a synergistic relationship become unlikely. Neither side is able to achieve a conclusion from negotiations in which both sides benefit.

Novices are restricted by fears, especially that they will be surprised or, at worst, ambushed. By that fact alone, any alternative offered by the other side must be considered hazardous. Because the opposing side is regarded as an enemy, he or she is seen as belligerent and aggressive, intimidating or manipulative. Any attempt to gain the opposer's confidence is often met with suspicion. The novice is reluctant to offer alternatives, assuming that if they haven't been considered prior to the negotiation, they can't be good.

Novices are without the ability to see through and anticipate conclusions of transactions. They do not understand the use of alternatives to reduce deadlock. Novices, in attempting to create a positive negotiating climate, may even try to use a truthful disclosure and tell what they will settle for. However, because novices appear incompetent, experienced negotiators think they are lying or do not know what they are saying. Novices are not listened to or taken seriously. Their opposers will not even attempt to evaluate what they are saying.

The first ability of competent sales negotiators is how to use all of their skills, even if only to neutralize the fears of the inexperienced. Competent

> Experience in negotiation alone does not make one competent.

salespeople are able to leave their opposers with the impression that they are fit, proper, able, and adequate. Their manners are composed, understanding, self-controlled, and realistic. Competent salespeople are easily recognized for their ability. Their verbal and nonverbal communication confirms the initial impression they have created. They are truthful, reliable, and have respect for the other person's point of view. They know the vocabulary, are aware of the issues, and know how to deal with the issues so that both sides benefit.

Competent sales negotiators know how to prepare for negotiation, how to set a climate (the negotiation environment), how to deal with limits, strategies, and tactics, how to do their homework, how to "read" gestures, how to listen to meta-talk (the hidden meanings of words), how to identify and use the strategy of changing levels, how to organize their material, and, in general, how to do all of these things *effectively*.

What differentiates a *master* negotiator from a competent one? A music critic once said that Haydn first taught Mozart how to write string quartets. Mozart then taught Haydn how string quartets should be written. This ability to surpass instruction is what differentiates the competent artist from the master artist. (It takes nothing away from Haydn's greatness to say this. Haydn himself, after hearing the first Mozart quartets, called him the greatest composer then living.) The master negotiator, in addition to being fit, proper, able, and adequate, not only possesses all the necessary instructed qualities of a negotiator but also has a personal philosophy with an ethical concern: one that can bring to a close a sales negotiation that is completely satisfactory to both sides.

The greatness of master sales negotiators lies in their selection of such a philosophy. There is, however, no single "right" way. Aristotle's ethical concern is revealed in *Rhetorica* (a study of the negotiation process of his day). He states, ". . . man has a sufficient natural instinct for what is true and usually does arrive at the truth. Hence, the man who makes a good guess at truth is likely to make a good guess at things that are true and things that just have a natural tendency to prevail over their opposites. . . ." Aristotle reaffirms his beliefs when he states, ". . . things that are true and things that are better are, by their nature, practically always easier to prove and easier to believe."

In the more than 2,300 years since Aristotle lived, perceptions have changed and grown. Although many still play a win-or-lose game (the essence of Greek tragedy), the master negotiator realizes that the tragic flaw of Greek heroes, *hubris* (overweening pride, arrogance), has no place in the intricate, interpersonal relationships of today.

In Aristotle's time and for centuries afterward, a person's role in society was rigidly defined according to rank. The ambitious were forced to play a win-or-lose game—often with lethal results to their rivals or themselves. Now, people in every facet of society have certain strengths they will not bargain away without a recompensing reward. Anyone may have to negotiate with business people, bureaucrats, professionals, sales and purchasing people, terrorists, muggers, petty thieves, even saints—the whole gamut of people in the world today. Can you hold out for an unconditional surrender? You may lose more than you can afford.

Your philosophy should facilitate negotiation. It should pass this test that if you experience it being used by an opposer, you will feel satisfaction.

> When your negotiation philosophy can be considered a building block in the human development process, not just a method of persuasion, you know that you are on the right track.

Sales Negotiation Contrasted

Sales negotiators do not have a one-track mind when they insist that most of life's transactions are in the nature of a sale. Even the simplest forms of life are firm "believers" in symbiosis: the intimate living together of two dissimilar organisms in a mutually beneficial relationship. It takes the higher forms of life to accentuate the negative and minimize the positive values of cooperation. Some even go so far as to bad-mouth their competitors' products in their efforts to sell their own.

Former Mayor Ed Koch of New York City did this on television in 1984 when he attacked an old rival, then Comptroller Harrison J. Goldin "Do you think there are many people who would buy one of our [New York City] notes if his name was on there instead of mine?" Unfortunately, the Mayor hadn't done his homework. Goldin's name was on the notes. Koch's wasn't. Both their names were on the city's bonds, so neither could claim credit for any extra sales. And, of course, the only names that mattered, the city's long-suffering taxpayers, didn't appear on either bonds or notes. Their only comfort (a cold one) was Goldin's counterattack on television: "What do you expect from a *yenta* who spends all of his time dumping on people ?" "We, the people," have grown accustomed to politicians who play win-or-lose games. We know who the loser was.

When producers want to know what the public wants, they graph it as curves. When they want to tell the public what to get, they say it in curves.

Marshall McLuhan, "Eye Appeal," *The Mechanical Bride*, 1951.

The Manipulative Salesperson

Lyndon B. Johnson's celebrated remark about a political opponent, "He can't walk and chew gum at the same time," plays on the easy contempt most people feel for the physically clumsy. Beneath the surface, however, lies a hidden doubt: "Can I walk and chew gum simultaneously?" A quick memory check usually provides the proper assurance and unforced laughter follows.

Even those rare human beings who can rub their tummies and pat their heads at the same time often come a cropper when they attempt to make real-life situations conform to a so-called sure-fire technique for making a sale. Its rules are considered to be timeless. In reality, sales concepts are considered constant in an unchanging world. They are regarded as a series of discreet decisions—traffic lights, if you will—that tell you whether to stop or go. This produces a splendid feeling of self-righteousness and a sureness that others can be manipulated "for their own good."

How well this concept works in a changing process world was graphically illustrated in 1983 in the course of a single week. Charles Z. Wick, a seller of ideas as director of the U.S. Information Agency, was asked at the 1983 winter meeting of the California Press Association to explain why Margaret Thatcher, then Britain's Prime Minister, had opposed the U.S. invasion of Grenada. Afterall, the United States had given whole-hearted support to Britain in its war with Argentina over the Falkland Islands. That war was very popular politically in Britain, just as the Grenada invasion was in the United States.

What Wick had forgotten, if indeed he had ever been informed, was that Thatcher, for political and moral reasons, had refused to yield to force and give up British territory in the Falklands. Grenada was something else. The Treaty of Paris (1783) had bestowed independence to the United States and awarded Grenada to Britain. The island gained complete independence in 1974 and became a full member of the Commonwealth of Nations.

Lacking this basic information, Wick began more than 200 years after the historical relation had started and offered an explanation for Thatcher's aberrant behavior. As a forethought he said: "Maybe I shouldn't say this publicly, and this is just my own personal opinion." Then, "Margaret Thatcher is a great Prime Minister. She's also a woman." Groans from the audience produced further afterthoughts. "She's a great lady. When I say she's a woman, I'm talking about people who are superior to men. Please don't print what I just said. I'll never get back to London." Perhaps not, but his words did. No sale. Wick's world was out of step with the times.

Once salespersons have agreed to act as agents, their only proper roles are to be salespersons of others' "final offers." Often they must rely on the "kindness of strangers," as Tennessee Williams put it, for satisfaction of their own needs.

> A sales agent with limited authority is never in an enviable position when it comes to decisions of what is the right or wrong move to make.

The *New York Times* (December 12, 1983) offered this example: Following a much trumpeted "strategic cooperation" agreement between Israel and the United States, a State Department official said, "The Arabs already believe the United States and Israel have an extremely close military relationship. Why upset the Arabs by drawing more attention to it?" We did, and they were.

In the midst of the storm, then Secretary of State Shultz tried to smooth over this *fait accompli*. He met for two and a half hours with King Hassan II of Morocco, who in the past had tried and failed to bring Jordan, the Palestinians, and Israel into negotiations on the basis of President Reagan's 1982 Middle East initiative. The *Times* gave this summary of the meeting: "According to Mr. Shultz, his talks with King Hassan this afternoon were 'constructive,' which an aide later said meant that the King was not abusive to Mr. Shultz." He was spared to peddle his wares another day.

When we have afterthoughts, many of us try to sell our consciences on our essential goodness:

- I did the right thing and I feel good.
- I did the wrong thing and I feel guilty.
- I did it, and I'm glad.

Despite the occasional discomfort that pangs of conscience cause us, it is nothing compared to the havoc created when morals are trimmed and fitted to sell our position to specialized audiences at a particular time.

The *Washington Post*, December 14, 1983, offered an extreme example of stop-and-go morality in reviewing the troubles encountered by Eli Lilly and Co. when it began to market a prescription arthritis medicine, Oraflex, in 1982. The following chronology is instructive:

Lilly failed to report 32 deaths of Oraflex users overseas to the Food and Drug Administration before the agency licensed the drug for sale in the United States.

On May 9, 1982, Lilly launched the drug with a $12 million media drive, held two press conferences, and distributed 6,100 press kits that won widespread publicity for Oraflex and created a heavy demand from arthritis sufferers.

Two days later the FDA said the press kits "minimized the drug's potential for adverse reactions . . . ." It said the kits were "less than ethical, false and misleading," and an invitation to the press to make exaggerated claims for the drug.

In November 1983, the son of an 81-year-old woman who had died after taking Oraflex won $6 million in punitive damages from Lilly. At the trial, Lilly's chairman and CEO defended the company for not reporting overseas deaths, because neither the law nor ethics required it. He said Lilly had discussed the press kits with the FDA, which "had no serious objections." "After the fact, I think they were as shocked as we were . . . at the way the media blew up their interpretations of Oraflex. In many of the media reports the word 'cure' appeared. This was shocking."

In a December 5, 1983, letter to stockholders, the chairman said that Lilly "went beyond the bounds of good practice in making claims for Oraflex." While the company did not intend to mislead the public, hindsight suggests that . . . "the lay press materials exceeded the bounds of a reasonable promotion."

Important Thoughts for Sales Negotiating Success

A true Everybody Wins® agreement is accomplished by knowing and practicing the skills and techniques of sales negotiating, which must take into consideration the needs and interests not only of the buyer and seller but also of all who might be affected by the results of the negotiation.

> Successful sales negotiating is a skill. Like all skills it can be learned, and it can be improved. It is not something you either have or don't have. Winning sales negotiators are trained, not born.

Negotiation is a human process that occurs whenever human beings, or the entities that we create—partnerships, corporations, or nations—come together and exchange ideas for the purpose of changing a relationship. We are, therefore, negotiating each and every time we consciously or unconsciously set out to interact and exchange ideas and information with others to have them either do something or refrain from doing something.

> The sales negotiation process often begins long before the parties actually meet.

Thorough preparation before the meeting or contact in a negotiation is an essential part of the sales negotiating process. Your preparation, in fact, is a lifelong experience, beginning with self-evaluation—that is, knowing your philosophy of life, your career expectations, what you seek from the pending sales negotiation, and how you react emotionally and intellectually to challenges and frustrations, to name just a few.

Along with self-evaluation, you must have awareness of the world as it is seen from both the buyer's and the seller's point of view. To obtain this information about your opposers' attitudes and styles, you must evaluate their business

> Remember, the people with whom you are negotiating, like yourself, have a tendency not to vary their negotiating style but to stick with what they think has worked in the past.

operations—their customer service policies, advertising philosophy, management style—and also their personal tastes, habits, hobbies, and backgrounds, as well as any other information you may be able to obtain and deem appropriate to any pending negotiation. With this in mind, an examination of an opposer's past negotiations can also provide important clues.

"Dispatch is the soul of business, and nothing contributes more to Dispatch than Method."

Lord Chesterton, Letter to his son, Feb. 5, 1750.

The following is designed to acquaint you with the order, relation, and structure of sales negotiating. Carefully followed as a blue print for future sales negotiations, it can act as a guide to assist you in future successful negotiations.

The first major area of concern is *Subject Matter*. Always try to get an agreement in advance about the subject matter of the negotiation. What is it, in general terms, that is going to be discussed, so that when the negotiation is concluded both parties gain? If there is disagreement on the subject matter, and if so, why? Is it subject to any rules, or does it contain limits? What might the rewards or benefits be? Are there any penalties?

It is also important at this stage to identify the parties involved. How many? Will there be others, who might constitute an audience? Are you dealing with agents and principals? What is the nature of their authority? At this stage, in studying the past negotiations of all of the parties involved, are there any patterns that can be revealed? Have they, in fact, implemented previous final agreements?

The next essential point is *Objectives*. Consider the advantages and disadvantages not only of your objectives but also of whatever the other side's objectives might be. Can you identify a broad range of objectives, namely, short-term gains, and if those are unobtainable, what kind of long-range objective can be met?

> Objectives, simply stated, are the desired results of the negotiation.

Fact-finding and *assumptions* are vital to the negotiation process, because they presuppose that in the preparation stage you have examined fully all of the information and facts that the other side will be relying on. Recognize, however, that what is a fact to you may not be a fact to the other side.

Actually, what both sides rely on are assumptions—that is, what each side believes the facts to be. Your assumptions, as theirs, are based on experience and education. Therefore, fact-finding or the examination of assumptions is an essential part of the negotiating process.

Often a great deal of time can be wasted in a negotiation because your opposers do not understand that fact-finding is assumption-making. Furthermore, they may not even recognize when each of you is talking about a different thing.

For this reason in the initial stage, a fact-finding and fact-understanding session is usually desirable. At that time, areas of agreement for fact-finding methods can be determined, leaving areas of disagreement for the next step in the negotiating process, which is the formulation of the issues.

The formulation of issues should, whenever possible, be directed at differences over matters of agreed-on assumptions. General opinions, judgments, accusations, and other statements, colored by emotions, impede the negotiating process. When they occur, reexamine your own assumptions and those of your opposer, and clarify the issues.

Smaller Is Better

One effective way of viewing assumptions is to break the problem into smaller parts. That is, separate monetary and non-monetary considerations or conditions that can be agreed upon from those that cannot. Emotion should be distinguished from fact-finding. For example, "Those terms are outrageous" can be countered by showing the facts and figures that result in the terms.

Remember, issues can be either real or fanciful. They might be introduced to reduce the opposition's demands as well as to set the stage for counter demands. They can provide room to move or to change. They save face for oneself or for the opposer and can provide an inducement or a lever to get support for another issue. When used to merely manipulate, they are likely to backfire.

Agendas are made up of the issues to be dealt with and discussed in the negotiating process. Understanding the use of agendas is important in the negotiating process because you should not feel tied to any set order of issues listed in a printed document. You can vary the order. The agenda itself is negotiable.

Eventually, in the order structure of the negotiating process, both parties have an opportunity to state their relative positions clearly. Your position in negotiation is the view you have taken on an issue or a group of issues. As you negotiate, you should test the firmness of the other party's position. To obtain movement or change, there are many techniques you can use:

- Release a trial balloon or use leaks and rumors to see what the reaction might be, or whether there might be a partial withdrawal from the original position.

- Change your position suddenly to see the other side's reaction. This is commonly done when people offer to split the difference. One can hold behind-the-scenes discussions, either directly with the opposer or with others they are associated with or listen to.

- Make direct inquiries, asking about the possibility of changing this point or dropping that one.

Negotiation is a process of movement. Therefore, when establishing your position in the preparation stage, determine what your essentials are. What are your opposer's essentials? What must you have? What do you believe your opposer, *must* have?

Concession or a change of position in a negotiation is tied into how one perceives the satisfaction or lack of satisfaction of one's needs: "What is it that I have to get out of the negotiation?" Therefore, successful negotiation can be accomplished by establishing what your own needs and goals are, as well as by being constantly aware of your opposer's needs. With this awareness, you can move your opposer to work toward the satisfaction of mutual needs in the course of position changes.

> The ultimate agreement must represent a gain for both sides—an "everybody wins" agreement.

Negotiating Strategies and Tactics

What you do in a negotiation to get the other side to react, to get them to move, and to cover the distance in the negotiation is what we call *Strategies and Tactics*. *Strategies* are long-term moves to achieve your objectives. *Tactics*, on the other hand, are short-term moves that implement your strategies.

Proper knowledge and application of negotiating skills and techniques require that you know the full extent of the available strategies and tactics. Strategies and tactics can be divided into three categories:

- "When" strategies and tactics depend upon time to achieve change in the negotiation.
- "How" strategies and tactics deal with methods.
- "Where" strategies and tactics deal with places used to achieve change in the negotiation.

The prepared negotiator understands what the strategies and tactics can accomplish by understanding a variety of real-life examples. Do not limit yourself to examples in your chosen field. Creative sales negotiation requires you to change levels and points of view. Your customers are not "products" from a single mold. Each has a unique combination of needs and experiences that you must understand. Learn all you can about the needs of kings and commoners, of babies and octogenarians, and continue to expand your list as long as you live. You never know when the information will come in handy.

Negotiation at the planning stage envisions the various strategies and tactics that may be most appropriate to the negotiation at hand. Be prepared to change your strategies and tactics as you observe and evaluate the opposer's reactions. Feedback mechanisms available to you are composed of nonverbal communication, such as body language, the intellectual content or meaning of the response, and the meta-talk, the hidden meaning of the verbal response.

Intentionally or unintentionally, we all create the physical and emotional *climates* that surround us. Good playwrights are skilled at "setting the stage"—at creating an environment in which the actions of the characters seem logical.

The master sales negotiator must understand the nature of and the differences between climates. What you say, how you say it, what you look like, and many other factors are involved in creating the climates during a negotiation. You have the opportunity to make people work with you in a supportive climate, or you can unknowingly create a negative and defensive climate that will block your success in negotiation.

> Climates are the feelings or environment that we or others create during the negotiating process.

Your ability to create and control the proper positive climate in a negotiation can be the determining factor in your success. Therefore, the number of possible climates, their division into positive or negative environments, and the individual components that make up the identifiable climates are a vital part of the negotiator's training.

Goals of a Master Negotiator

There is no easy road for a master negotiator. It takes training and dedication, as well as constant application. Here are some characteristics of master negotiators:

- They view negotiation as a continuing life process in which no issue is irrevocably closed, even after agreements are reached and papers are signed. Changing life's circumstances may warrant additional effort.

- They have open minds. They are aware of their personal and business needs and equally aware of the other side's needs. They are flexible and able to establish mutual goals and interests quickly. Master negotiators do not try to persuade opposers that their views are wrong and should be changed. They do present creative alternatives that truly meet the other side's needs.

- They are cooperative, because cooperation creates mutual problem solving to achieve harmony. They are competitive because competition brings out differences that they use to discover mutually desired benefits.

Master negotiators, finally, view the negotiation process as one that satisfies the needs of both buyer and seller. Negotiation must not, however, meet only the goals of the individual on each side. It must also contribute to the well-being of the organizations they work for and the society in which they live—a truly "everybody wins" solution.

Key Points

"Many are called, but few are chosen" is true of many career choices, but no career is more demanding than that of the master negotiator. Sales negotiation is a *process*, so be prepared to move from (1) novice to (2) competent salesperson to (3) master negotiator. Then when you are trained to sharpen your skills, if you can develop a personal philosophy with an ethical concern, you are ready for Big Sales.

Belief in your assumptions is what makes a "fact" a fact—to you. But not necessarily to your opposer. Strategies and tactics, used wisely, help you move a negotiation to a conclusion in which everybody wins. Supportive climates help produce the results the master negotiator strives for.

Remember:

- Preparation is essential.
- Understanding needs can bring results you need.
- Have an end goal that everyone will want to implement.

Looking at
the Whole
Picture

Looking at the Whole Picture

I have always recognized that the object of business is to make money in an honorable manner. I have endeavored to remember that the object of life is to do good.

Peter Cooper, Speech at reception in his honor, 1874

Most salespeople worthy of the title did not enter the selling field because they thought it would be the easiest way to make money or felt it was necessarily the best they could hope to do. They went in because they rejected self-imposed limitations on their ambitions. They were willing to take risks, push themselves to higher and higher performance levels, create new opportunities for growth, and know the feeling of success.

There are still a few who describe those who meet their goals effortlessly as "born" salespeople—born lucky and born at the right time. In other words, they are "naturally" good at selling. Anyone who believes that should be forced to write Mae West's remark 100 times: "Goodness had nothing to do with it."

To those of you who shrink from trying because you feel you have been left behind, who think you cannot sell effectively because the buyer knows more about his company's product than you know about yours, who are sure the buyer will "win" on price and other conditions of the sale, take heart. You're not a terminal case—you just have a great deal to learn.

Archimedes said, "Give me where to stand and I will move the earth." All he needed was a lever long enough and a fulcrum strong enough. You are playing a win-or-lose game when you attempt to move the buyer with a lever and fulcrum, not to meet her needs but to satisfy your own.

What should you do? Stop thinking you can force your way (winning) from one move to the next. Learn that the right moves can be planned in advance. Study them carefully. Think them through. Plan alternatives in advance. Don't assume you will always, or even often, get your way. Discover what your real needs are, but give equal—or better, more— time to consideration of the buyer's needs. Forget about being a salesperson, a unisex term coined in 1901. We all concede you are a person. Why not change your conception of your occupation? Call yourself a "master negotiator"—a newer concept and occupation.

What is Sales Negotiation?

Sales negotiation is a skill that is applied to a specific profession. Like all skills, sales negotiation can be learned, refined, and constantly improved. It is based upon the Art of Negotiating® and is capable of being applied successfully to many of your life situations.

A few years ago, the president of a large, successful conglomerate came up to me after a seminar on negotiating mergers and acquisitions. He said, "Jerry, we've been doing pretty well this year, and there isn't much you can tell me about negotiating for mergers and acquisitions. We know how to acquire other companies. But you did teach me something today—that the same negotiating techniques I was using in my business dealings I could apply to my personal problems. For example, I had a disagreement with my son before I left this morning, and he told me some unkind things that I could do with my whole conglomerate. Now I realize I've got a lot more negotiating to do."

A Negotiating Philosophy:
The Sales Tool

We all have a negotiating philosophy, whether we are aware of it or not. One of the strongest forces in choosing one course of action over another is our philosophy. Master negotiators understand the use of a problem-oriented philosophy. They view their prospects' problems as mutual problems. They want to plan with their clients, not for them. They also realize that both parties are acting in a broader context. They know it is not enough that both become winners. Everybody must win.

Negotiating is a process that involves everyone. Successful negotiation requires not only facility but also a strength and excellence of moral purpose—not preconceived ideas of good and evil, but insights into the beneficial and lasting results. Only an all-satisfying agreement can achieve real permanence.

An editorial that appeared in The *Washington Post* on June 7, 1984, describing a master negotiator making his big sale, says it better than any abstract statement can:

> In the smoke, fire and litter of some of the worst rioting Washington experienced immediately after Martin Luther King, Jr.'s, assassination in 1968, there stood in one particularly fiery block a prominently untouched store: a supermarket, obviously skipped by the plunderers on this lawless night in the capital. It was a Giant store, and residents with local roots knew why it had been bypassed. Giant's ties with the city and with its neighbors and customers had always been strong, and in this store, the manager was a black man—an important "first" in those days. And Giant's special recognition of local responsibilities could be traced to its founder, Nehemiah M. Cohen, who died Tuesday at 93 after being injured in an auto accident four days earlier.

The story of Mr. Cohen—native of Jerusalem, ordained rabbi, one-time school teacher, sometime farmer and visionary storekeeper is about exceptional commercial and civic commitment to this region. Teaming up with a business acquaintance whose family owned a food distributorship in Pennsylvania, Mr. Cohen left the three small grocery stores he owned in Lancaster, Pa. to open the first Giant on Georgia Avenue during the Depression.

Steady growth, nurtured by Mr. Cohen's personal managerial style, turned one store into a thriving chain that today operates 132 stores and is the 12th largest retailer in the United States. Though internal feuding at one time threatened to immobilize Giant, Mr. Cohen's presence continued to be felt both inside and outside the firm. There was an accent on profitable operations, but with a strong emphasis on activity in, with and for local Washington.

Formal recognition of this activity came often, but was appreciated most by Mr. Cohen in 1974, when he received the Shem Tov Award of Adas Israel Congregation here, for exemplifying the highest ideals of good citizenship and for caring for others. *Mr. Cohen had stressed a personal philosophy that Giant had an obligation to repay the region it serves.*

It has been this spirit that saw Giant build a bright new supermarket in the heart of the Shaw neighborhood at a time when other chains were closing stores in the city. That spirit led to a longtime, still-standing sponsorship of school programs, and recognized neighborhoods in hiring practices. That supermaarket was, and still is, a rich legacy to be cherished by all of Washington, from a man who liked to share.

Negotiating Climates Make Sales

All of the climates and feelings that we experience in the negotiating process are of our own making. To some, this may seem unfair. It may even prompt a defense: "My problem is that the prospect has a problem." Of course. That is how you got your foot in the door in the first place. How you handle the problem is up to you. The successful negotiator has done her homework. She understands the problem, shares the buyer's concern about solving it, and by establishing a supportive climate is able to negotiate a mutually satisfactory solution. The salesperson with merely a game-oriented philosophy views the prospect as an adversary—someone who must be controlled or manipulated. If you are trying to push or control your prospect, you will only increase the defenses and decrease your chances of making a sale. The prospect will be armed—by you—with two alternatives: break off communications or play to make you the loser.

If you are accusing, judgmental, correcting, or indoctrinating, you will most likely create a defensive prospect. For example, if you tell a prospect that your product is the best that can be bought, you are trying to impose a subjective value judgment on him. The probable result is a

> Remember, customers want to learn. They resist being taught.

defensive climate. On the other hand, you can create a supportive climate by sticking to the descriptive terms: "Our product is currently used nationwide by 50,000 customers." Let the customer appraise your information. Don't do it for him. What if the prospect starts out being defensive? After all, it's her negotiation too. Do you let her control it? Of course not. You resent being controlled just as much as she does. Remember, it is much easier to change someone who is being defensive by responding with a supportive climate than by reinforcing her defensiveness with your own. When you hit a tennis ball over the net, the kind of spin you put on the ball determines the type of return shot you are going to get. It's the same with negotiating climates. The type of climate you create determines the type of climate you are going to get.

Dos and Don'ts for Master Selling and Buying Climates

1. *Do* be open-minded about your strategies and tactics. Be sure the words you use to describe them are essentially neutral. The way you use them will determine how successful you are in establishing a positive climate. Don't use them as fixed rules that determine who will be the winner. Instead, use them to move the sales negotiation forward toward a mutually satisfactory solution.

2. *Don't* attempt to manipulate with your body language. Unless you are a great actor you'll never get away with it. However, be aware of the meaning of your prospect's gestures and gesture clusters. They give you valuable information about the progress of the negotiation, even if the prospect is trying to manipulate you. In that case, you can recognize the way he or she wants you to go, and you can make an informed decision about the direction you should take. Read your own gestures to understand your present feelings. If you don't like what they show about your feelings, you can change them, for example, from being defensive to being supportive.

3. *Do* be conscious of clichés. For example, "Let me be honest with you" implies you have been anything *but* in the past. You

> If you discover yourself using clichés, quickly change the course of your thoughts.

are relying too much on stock phrases, which may very well be false or at least appear to be false. If the buyer is using apparently false clichés, don't correct him. Recognize the needs that he is unconsciously revealing, and move quickly to satisfy them. That's what you're there for.

4. *Do* use questions to establish your prospect's needs, to clarify issues, and to advance creative alternatives. Effective questions channel thoughts, guide the discussion, and lead to greater understanding. Avoid rhetorical questions. They often create anxiety. (How can anyone say that we don't have a good product? Why would anyone question our reliability?)

5. *Do* listen carefully. You've spent a lot of time framing the "right" question. Be sure to get full value from your effort Avoid interruptions or contradictions. Evaluate the information you have received before you respond.

6. *Don't* propose either/or alternatives. All too often they offer "first the good news, then the bad" choices. This is a common form of manipulation. Instead, develop creative alternatives. Rather than, "If you have to ask the price, you can't afford it," develop new positives: improved delivery, group price, package deal, extended terms, custom design, extra service, different deposits, customized payment plan, insurance for unknown losses, prevention of risks through new guarantees, and so on.

7. *Don't* impose artificial limits, such as self-doubt, on your creativity. Test your creative thinking by changing levels and/or points of view, but don't be afraid of thinking the "unthinkable." Be on your way to becoming a master negotiator. You will then be able to handle any transaction for any amount.

A Checklist of Negotiation Skills

I. Understanding the barriers to communication that are self-made.

   A. Communicating effectively between two people (Methods are listed in order of approximate efficiency.)

Nonverbal

1. Work alongside, guide, use participative experiments, handle materials together.

2. Use models and demonstrations, act out skits, and so on.

3. Draw diagrams, isolate key points, use graphs. (see #4)

4. Use pictures: motion pictures, slides, photos, paintings, posters, scrapbooks.

5. a. Use body language, gestures, kinesics.

    b. Paralinguistics (volume, tone, noises that are not formal language but are indicating an attitude).

Verbal

6. Recall experiences in common, news items, examples, illustrations on many levels of experience.

7. Use case histories—concrete situations in story form.

8. Employ operational talk-actional language, functional language, relational language.

9. Generalize—use abstract words, few references, categorized ideas, only high-level abstractions.

10. Write only one-way communications, limit feedback. No one method is "best"—each benefits from being used in combination with the rest.

B. Barriers-self-made, unconsciously erected

    1. Selective listening

    2. Hidden assumptions

3. Rationalizations

4. Displacements

5. Repressions

6. Self-image

7. Loaded words

C. How to improve your listening skill

> The process of communication, relying upon multiple functions, must, of necessity, be ambiguous and, in so being, serves many different purposes.

1. Pay close attention to the speaker's opening and closing statements. Construct a mental "word map" for the content in between.

2. You will be a better listener if you pay as much attention to the speaker's nonverbal communication as you do to his verbal communication.

3. A good listener not only motivates a person to talk but also to listen to his own words, which can lead to emotional catharsis and self-understanding. When listening takes place, parties open up.

4. Nondirective listening is the most helpful. The listener absorbs all information offered, but makes no attempt to respond or guide the conversation.

5. The moment we begin to offer advice, our listening loses its nondirective quality—and also its effectiveness.

6. The nondirective listener listens to what is said for understanding and without evaluation.

D. Suggestions for becoming a nondirective listener

1. Take time. If you feel that someone is troubled and needs to talk, listen with attention. It is not a waste of time. If you can help him clear his mind, you will also clarify later communication between the two of you.

2. Be understanding. If the speaker becomes extremely emotional, let it pass until exhausted. Show you understand and that you feel the subject is important.

> Do not oppose force, but step aside and let it pass. It will then dissipate.

3. Limit your verbal reactions. While the speaker continues to talk, confine yourself to what has been called a series of "eloquent and encouraging grunts" (Humm, Oh, or I see.) If the speaker pauses, say nothing. A nod or other nonverbal form of feedback may encourage her to continue.

4. Do not attempt to evaluate what has been said. Remember, there are no absolutes, especially in an emotional situation.

5. Do not give guidance, even if asked to do so. The speaker is searching for his own creative solution. He is not ready for yours.

6. In retrospect, analyze the information you have received in different ways—changing levels vertically (different positions of authority) and horizontally (different points of view), to see how it might apply to your own problems and growth.

> Remember, you can learn as much, if not more, from "losers" as you can from "winners." This is what makes these terms so meaningless to a good listener.

7. Silence is the listener's strength and skill. Jesse Nirenberg in _Getting Through to People_ deals with five human characteristics that work against a meeting of minds.

a.   Many people are conservative in outlook and tend to resist change in the status quo. Since the purpose of negotiation is to change relationships, this characteristic can be a serious impediment to the negotiation process.

b.   As we have seen, most of us have a tendency to think our own thoughts rather than to listen.

c.   We are inclined to listen selectively, hearing only what we want to hear.

d.   Some people are habitually secretive and suspicious of the motives of others.

e.   As already noted, hidden assumptions often are an important factor in a breakdown of communication.

E. Overcoming communication barriers

1.   Be sure that ideas alone do not dominate the conversation. Honest expression of emotion can be persuasive.

2.   Use questions to focus the opposer's attention, and learn his thoughts.

3.   Be alert to the opposer's reactions. How you say it is as important as what you say.

4.   Make sure your opposer understands the purpose of your conversation from the very beginning.

5.   Help your opposer examine her assumptions.

F.   Other considerations

1.   Questions are an effective way of drawing out people's thoughts by demanding a response—if well-thought-out and skillfully phrased, they make the giving of information an enjoyable experience.

2. Summarize by asking another question ("Then you think that . . . ?").

3. Emotions: People do not feel strongly about things that are unimportant to them.

> Emotions are vital clues to discovering what your opposer's needs are. Encourage the expression of emotions.

G. How to keep people's attention when negotiating

1. Allow the right time for the discussion.

2. Stay with the idea.

3. Be succinct, and concise.

4. Don't develop verbal tics.

5. Keep bringing in new and additional material as you move the negotiation.

6. Use words and ideas close to reality (abstractions hinder, not help).

II. From my studies and research: reading and responding to body language.

A. The emotional attitudes of opposers are communicated nonverbally.

B. They indicate his or her feelings and, therefore, his or her negotiating position.

C. Nonverbal messages must be considered in the context of the environment and time when they occur.

D. Gestures are considered together, as gesture clusters. They signify emotional attitudes: protective, uncertain, aggressive, honesty, reassurance, cooperative, confident, holding back, openness, suspicion.

E. It is important to consider nonverbal communication with verbal messages—they should be consistent with each other. Inconsistency may indicate hidden motivations, feelings, or needs. A change may be needed in your negotiating approach.

III. Understanding and using hidden verbal meaning

A. Meta-talk beyond talk—tip-offs to the real meanings.

B. Analyze meta-talk

1. Examine what your opposer does not say.

2. Trite and routine expressions:

a. Throwaway phrases ("By the way," "Before I forget?")

b. "To tell the truth," "honestly."

c. Opposer repeats your question (to gain time).

d. "Do you see what I mean?"

e. "I'll try my best."

3. To detect hidden meanings, change relationships (imagine same words said in different setting with different players)

C. Classifications of meta-talk (cliches):

1. Hiding the halo. "In my humble opinion. . . ."

2. Arrogance and false modesty. "As you well know. . . ."

3. Softeners. "I venture to say. . . ."

4. Foreboders. "Nothing is wrong. . . ."

5. Continuers. "What else is new?"

6. Interesters. "And do you know what he said?"

7. Downers. "Are you happy now?"

8. Convincers. "Doesn't everybody?"

9. Strokers. "I like it very much but. . . ."

10. Pleaders. "I try my best."

11. Understanding and using needs. "I didn't go too far did I?"

D. Meta-talk and gestures combine to form attitudes and relationships. All add to communication.

E. Meta-talk should be avoided in negotiations. Use of it prevents clear, sincere communication.

F. Knowledge of meta-talk is an advantage, enabling you to understand opposer's needs, hidden assumptions, the type of climate he creates, and how to relate to them.

IV. Using questions to direct the negotiation

A. Questions create anxiety and depend for effectiveness upon:

1. Timing (when)

2. Method (how)

3. Content (what)

B. Objective: to achieve clarification and understanding. Therefore, it should be simple, straightforward, and designed to serve the relationship.

C. Five functions of questions:

1. Cause attention.

2. Get information.

3. Give information.

4. Start the other person thinking.

5. Bring to a conclusion (close).

D. Questions are an integral part of the negotiation process and are a means of implementing strategies and tactics.

E. The Question Map

Start _____ Finish

Function I Questions	Function II Questions	Function IV Questions	Function V Questions
1. _____	1. _____	1. _____	1. _____
2. _____	2. _____	2 _____	2 _____
3. _____	3. _____	3. _____	3. _____

This map represents an entire negotiation from start to close, no matter how long the time involved—three hours, three days, or three weeks.

Function I. Question: Gain attention. "How are you?" "How's your golf these days?"

Function II. Question: Get information. "When will it be delivered?" "How much will it cost?"

Function III. Questions not used, because they are too controlling.

(Do not use Function III questions to give information because they cause antagonism in negotiations. They are more useful in cross-examinations.)

Function IV. Question: Start the other person thinking.

Function V. Question: Close. Once you have this map laid out in advance with the questions you are going to ask, you can sit back and relax, carefully observing all that is going on. You can close when appropriate. You can also delay closing until another time if the other party is not ready: "What day next week do you want to see my technical people?"

Key Points

Master negotiation requires the assumption of big responsibilities as well as big rewards, not all of them monetary. "To be or not to be" is a question that a master negotiator never need ask.

Sharpen Your Skills and Attitudes:

- Your negotiating philosophy
- The climate you make
- Communication barriers—recognizing and surmounting barriers
- Listening
- Body language
- Learn to understand and use meta-talk
- Questions

What to Look Out For— Portrait of the No-Sale

3

What to Look Out For— Portrait of the No-Sale

3

"Every portrait that is painted with feeling is a portrait of the artist, not of the sitter."

Oscar Wilde, The Picture of Dorian Gray, 1892

In our attempts to gain guidance from past attitudes, we get very little help when we consider society's image of salespeople and negotiators. Let us look at some of these.

To the Editor of *The New York Times*:

In an editorial entitled "The Action of Truth" (June 20), you expressed a bit of fiction of your own when you wrote, "Some mongers of mere fact, notably salesmen and politicians, routinely pretend to be revealing truth."

I do not object to your grouping salesmen with politicians, for both must sell their ideas to survive and were it not for the creation of sales, the entire economy would collapse. I do, however, regret on behalf of the 50,000 salespeople we represent the characterization that we "routinely pretend to be revealing truth." Are you, Sir, calling America's salesmen liars?

May I inform you that modern American salesmen depend upon the good will of their customers. Their word is their bond. Do not confuse praise of one's own product with lying.

In every group there are those who fall below the standard, but to paint all who sell for a living with the same brush is to do violence to all the ideals of The Times. You stand foursquare for truth, and salesmen have the right to expect you to be guided by your own high standards.

Marvin Leffler, chairman, National Council of Salesmen's Organizations, Inc. New York, July 9,1984.

An old slogan of the *New York Times*, "All the news that's fit to print," would seem to place the newspaper high on the list of "mongers of mere fact," however noble their objective. At the same time, people who must sell their ideas to survive make up a vast portion of the people who work for a living. The fact that they do survive proves their competence. But a traditional image of the salesman—or salesperson, if you will—gets in the way of the truth.

For example:

"Women who hate the idea of selling," says David King, founder of Careers for Women, "soon discover that it isn't actually selling that they hate. Rather, they hate their image of what a salesman is." This image, he says, is "some dreadful combination of 'Avon Calling' and Willy Loman dying."

Barbara Pletcher, founder of the California-based National Association for Professional Saleswomen (NAPS), compares the image to a "composite of the 'Music Man,' a snake oil dealer and a horse trader . . . with a callous disregard for the welfare of others." The image problem has, according to King and Pletcher, kept a lot of women out of a lot of money and a good route to the board room.

"It's a fact," says King, "that more women will enter the executive boardroom through the 'sales' door than from graduate programs in law and business combined."

"The thing that frustrated me," says Pletcher, who once sold Sunbeam appliances and taught marketing for eight years, "was that none of my students were interested in selling positions, and most of the good jobs when you leave campus are in sales."

Pletcher, 37, wrote *Saleswoman: A Guide to Career Success*, to encourage women to get out of staff positions, where "rewards are based on attendance, seniority, appearances, politics . . ." and to go for "line positions where you are fighting the battles for the organization" and where performance is directly measurable.

(From *Careers: Birth of the Saleswoman*, by Marta Vogel, The *Washington Post*, May 17, 1984.)

Most of us, salespeople or not, have been guilty of practicing certain selling techniques that help perpetuate the myth that selling is not among the most reputable of careers.

Here are some of the reasons:

We *coax*. Gentle flattery is used to nudge buyers into action. We *urge* or *cajole*, usually to get buyers out of or into something. We *wheedle* or *persuade*, using kindness and patience. We *manipulate*. Buyers realize (too late) how artfully and fraudulently they have been had. All of these techniques are blatant appeals to emotion without regard for the needs of buyers. For example, here is some of the old "standard" sales wisdom, using these techniques.

Out-of-Date Persuasion Techniques

I. Present *strongest* arguments *first*, if listeners are little interested in your message, to arouse their interest.

II. Present *lesser points first*, if listeners are already interested.

III. Bring out *negative points* (as well as positive) when dealing with:

A.   Educated people.

B.   People who disagree at the outset.

C.   People who are exposed to negative argument from others.

IV. *Do not* bring out negative points when people:

A.   Are uneducated.

B.   Agree with you at the start.

C.   Are not likely to be exposed to outside counterarguments.

V.   Primary effect: What a person hears *first* lingers with him *longest*.

VI. Let listeners draw *their own* conclusions if the proposition involves them *personally* (for example, their opinions of themselves).

VII. When the idea is an *impersonal* one (for example, a new method or material), listeners will welcome conclusions drawn by the speaker.

VIII. Let listeners draw *their own* conclusions if the benefits of the idea are *obvious*. (If these benefits are *not immediately obvious* or if the subject matter is complex, spell out the benefits in detail.)

IX. The use of *fear* as a persuasive tactic.

A.   Positive (four states):

1.   Listeners grow tense.

2.   "This might happen to me."

3.   Tension is reduced as they hear how to avoid the threat.

4.   Reduced tension acts as reinforcement of the speaker's recommendation.

B.   Negative (pitfalls):

1.   If too much anxiety is created, listeners will automatically tune you out.

2. If a threat exceeds the listeners' tolerance, they may react hostilely toward you as the source of the threat.

    a. They will refuse to believe your statements.

    b. They will form a personal dislike for you and your company.

3. Listeners will experience a psychological blackout. They will "forget" to remember.

4. They will lose interest in the subject, or deny the importance of the threat.

X. Get listeners into the act. Get them to repeat (or write) all or part of your argument in their own words. *The simple act of saying will influence their private convictions.*

Most Americans equate sales negotiation with compromise. There is so much confusion over this term that it is usually followed by "using the carrot *or* the stick." To set the record straight, the term is "carrot and the stick." If you want a mule to walk for you, put a carrot on the end of a stick and hold it in front of him. Then your mule will walk. There is an Arabic saying, "If weak, compromise—if strong, no need to compromise."

Americans tend to make a virtue out of necessity. When we compromise, it is usually at the end of a long, hard session. Everyone is bloody. All are losers because all have been forced to relinquish, and none have gained. Not only that, but the result is temporary. No one wants to honor the agreement unless continually forced. There is also a feeling that to compromise means a loss of character, rights, or principles.

A close kin of compromise is accommodation. Here one side does all of the compromising and waits to get even. Another tactic is conciliation. Its theme song is "I Surrender, Dear." Benjamin Disraeli stated it well when he said, "If you are not very clever, you should be conciliatory."

Another approach is:

"Ours is the country where, in order to sell your product, you don't so much point out its merits as you first work like hell to sell yourself."

Louis Kronenberger, Company Manners, 1954.

All of these prescriptions for "sure-fire" sales can probably work some of the time, but usually for only a very short time. If you are an opportunist, you may think of them as an advantage. If, instead, you are looking for long-term gains, forget about them. In an article reviewing the decline and fall of Continental Illinois National Bank, The Washington Post (July 29, 1984) quoted a lending officer of a rival bank: "I know most of what happened. But I don't know why it happened. And I'm sometimes not even sure it happened." Don't let this be your epitaph as a salesperson.

Practitioners of manipulation are not as confused as their opposers often are. Manipulators know exactly what they want—to win big. Each encounter with a potential buyer is a challenge to a win-or-lose game. They intend to win.

Helen Keller said, "Security is mostly a superstition. It does not exist in nature, nor do the children of men as a whole experience it. Avoiding danger is no safer in the long run than outright exposure. Life is either a daring adventure or nothing." While it is true that win-or-lose game players compulsively seek risks to affirm their superiority, Helen Keller's inspiring life lends a different interpretation to her words.

William James comes close to pointing up this difference: "It is only by risking our persons from one hour to another that we live at all. And often enough our faith beforehand in an uncertified result is the only thing that makes the result come true."

Making the Big Sale

That is the difference between a Willy Loman and a master negotiator—the negotiator makes and continues to make the big sales. The Willy Lomans of the world have no faith in anything, not even in themselves. The only thing they are sure of is that life is a gamble, a series of unrelated episodes in which the "best man" wins.

While giving a seminar for a group of purchasing agents in London, I was told this story of a win-or-lose game: A salesman came to a buyer's office to tell about his company's products. The purchasing agent asked the salesman to begin his presentation. With that, the salesman took out his flip chart, put it on the agent's desk, and began talking while flipping the chart. After three flips, the agent arose from his seat, hit the flip chart hard with his hand, and sent it flying to the far wall. The shocked salesman left the room without a word and returned to his sales office. An hour later, the purchasing agent received a call from the sales manager asking for an explanation of his strange behavior. The agent explained that long before, he had promised himself that after one hundred salespeople had flipped charts indiscriminately at him, he would behave just as he did that day. He had nothing against the salesman. It was just that the salesman's number was up and he lost.

The master negotiator sees the world differently. Life is not a series of discreet moves, each of which produces a live winner and a dead loser. Instead, it is a process in which each move involves risks to both sides. However, the risks are worth taking because of a faith that in a successful negotiation, "everybody wins."

Key Points

Anyone who professes to tell the truth, the whole truth, and nothing but the truth is lying. Many competent salespeople, rightly or wrongly, have a reputation for being "less than honest" when, in fact, they are suffering from self-imposed limitations.

Sales techniques that work upon buyers' emotions rather than upon their needs are like a hambone without ham. They add some flavor to the soup but no substance. There is no such thing as a surefire sale, unless both buyer and seller are ignited by the desire to satisfy their needs and the everexpanding pie that makes up our society.

Coming In Out of the Cold: The Realities of Negotiation

4

Coming In Out of the Cold: The Realities of Negotiation

"Seest thou a man diligent in his business? He shall stand before kings; he shall not stand before mean men."

Old Testament, Prov. 22:29

The celebrated cliché, "The Greeks had a word for it," implies that every action, no matter how naughty, can be precisely labeled. The English language is more ambiguous. Take the verb, "to sell." It covers a multitude of sins, such as sell out, sell your birthright, sell your soul or your vote, sell short, sell down the river. It can also be used as a synonym for betray or cheat. And of course you've heard the one about the traveling salesman.

A more sober and neutral definition of sell is to give up property to another for money or other valuable consideration. The following is an amplification of this definition from the traditional marketing expert's point of view:

Selling: Many customer purchases are due to product promotion. In these cases, buyers have decided what to buy without any persuasion on the part of the sales personnel. However, when the consumer is comparison shopping or is purchasing expensive home furnishings or appliances, he often seeks specific suggestions from a salesperson to help choose a style or a specific brand of a product. Retailers, wholesalers, and purchasing managers of manufacturers also need help from salesmen. Manufacturers' salesmen inform them of new products and the market reaction to them. These salesmen also take buyers' orders and assume responsibility for the delivery of the merchandise.

That's it. Period. As a poet said about another universal "truth": "That is all ye know on earth, and all ye need to know." Following quite naturally from this point of view is Arthur Miller's description in *Death of a Salesman* (1949):

> Willy was a salesman. And for a salesman there is no rock bottom to the life. He don't put a bolt to a nut, he don't tell you the law or give you medicine. He's a man way out there in the blue, riding on a smile and a shoeshine. And when they start not smiling back that's an earthquake. And then you get yourself a couple of spots on your hat, and you're finished.

Both of these "portraits" of salespeople, especially Miller's, are all too real. They do exist in real life, and in great numbers. It would be comforting to think of them as caricatures but, in truth, they are stereotypes, frozen in time by self-imposed limitations. Miller's Willy Loman fits Talleyrand's description of the Bourbon kings: "They have learned nothing and forgotten nothing." The marketing point of view presented the salesperson as a mere ordertaker.

How to Make a Climate Work

Whether we recognize it or not, every sales negotiation has a "prevailing temper" or climate. The level of achievement produced by negotiators is most clearly the result of their ability to control the type of climate in which they operate.

A Willy Loman, unchanged by life experiences, makes no attempt to control the negotiating climate. Seeing situations only in black or white, he either will feel helpless and dependent, leaving to the opposers by default the choice of a climate, or, from fear of change and/or out of ignorance, will insist on having only his way considered. ("I will hold my breath until I turn blue if I don't get my way." "What worked once will always work.")

The usefulness of a positive attitude rather than a negative one has become apparent to master negotiators. Therefore, they are willing to create a positive climate. But sometimes they inadvertently step over the boundary line between a positive climate and one that is perceived by the other side as a manipulative one. In most cases this is not a conscious decision. They only wish to expedite matters and try to impose the "best" solution on their

> Master negotiators understand the need for a resolution to the problem. They see themselves in an active, rather than a passive, role.

opposer. They may place more value on "helping" and saving time than on reaching a mature solution to a mutual problem.

Jack Gibb in *Is Help Helpful?* explores some of the possible boobytraps of attempting to speed up a negotiation:

"Depending upon his own needs and upon the way he sees the motives of the helper, the recipient will have varied reactions. He may feel gratitude, resentment, or admiration. He may feel helpless and dependent, or jealous of the helper who has the strength or resources to be in the helper role. He may feel indebted or pressured to conform to the preconceived demands or beliefs of the helper."

Salespersons who are not too competent can fail to create a positive, supportive climate because they are not aware that an opposer's particular needs vary almost from moment to moment, and a shift in needs can create a shift in climate.

The Pseudosupportive Stance (attempts at being supportive). Many negotiators in attending The Art of Negotiating® seminars often express puzzlement that despite their best efforts to create a supportive climate, they have elicited reactions ranging from suspicion to outright hostility.

The 1972 Arkansas Democratic Primary race between Senator J. William Fulbright and Dale Bumpers sheds some light on this problem. Bumper's campaign strategy was to adopt a pseudosupportive stance toward the veteran senator's positions. He "only" reminded the voters that they had lost faith in the government and felt it was time for a change.

Fulbright was reduced to impotent rage. "Can it mean that you have found nothing in my record of the last 30 years with which you disagree? I'm not infallible. Why can't you be negative?" No wonder many opposers, engulfed by a "supportive" climate, react, first, with suspicion, and then, with anger.

> Another common error of some negotiators is the use of pseudoclimates as crutches to sustain negotiations that might otherwise collapse.

Other Pseudoclimates. Pseudoclimates are designed to give the appearance of pressing "nonnegotiable" demands while behind the scenes, old-fashioned horse trading is going on.

Negotiations between municipal labor unions and New York City officials regularly supply fine examples of pseudoclimates created with badly gnawed scenery. After weeks of posturing, a strong, confident mayor and a troupe of tough, unyielding labor leaders announce agreement and quickly bring down the curtain before the taxpayers can begin to scream for their money back.

Unfortunately, pseudoclimates produce pseudoagreements. The only thing agreed to is that both sides (in this case, city government and labor leaders) have emerged with their power intact. However, none of the issues that concern taxpayers and union members are any closer to settlement than they were before the negotiation.

Similar scenes are acted out daily throughout the United States, not only in public affairs but in private industry as well. What is wrong with this type of negotiation? After all, both sides get just about all they can reasonably expect, and the status quo is preserved for a while longer.

A pseudoclimate, probably more prevalent in failed marriages than in business affairs, involves withholding.

> The chief flaw in this pseudoclimate is that the longer it is sustained, the greater the expectations of the victim and the greater the potential for disappointment.

Withholding possesses both passive and negative qualities and has one essential requirement—the withholder must have something that another person wants badly. Then that person can be manipulated.

Both sides, in fact, are being unrealistic. Neither has made the least attempt to understand the other. Again, the basic needs of both sides are left unsatisfied.

Create a Positive Climate

Master negotiators—makers of the big sales—use the negotiating process fully. They are truly positive. They are critical, realistic, and cognizant of the weaknesses and strengths of both sides, in essence, "honest," a much abused word that deserves to be refurbished, rethought, and revived.

Richard Rhodes, in a *New York Times* article, gave some examples of how fundamental equality can be built into a system:

> When cattlemen agree to sell cattle to one another, they also agree which of them shall do the weighing. If the buyer does the weighing, he is obliged to pay a higher price per pound. If the seller does the weighing, the buyer pays less. Similarly, when cattlemen arrange to divide the herd, they agree that one of them will work the cutting gate and the other will have first choice of the half he wants.

These systems recognize that no matter how hard we may try to be objective and impartial in our judgments, we are no more likely to achieve absolute truth than any of the philosophers have. Even to arrive at a limited "truth," we must help create a positive climate and system that are able to enlist the confidence of all participating negotiators. With a mutual effort of this sort, much practical good can come from a deal. Without it, very few lasting results can be achieved.

Key Points

The significance of a man is not in what he attains, but rather in what he longs to attain.

Kahlil Gibran

In attempting to use skills such as creating climates, we must be fully involved, prepared to take chances, depend on our creativity and not on manipulation, and trust our ability to make positive climates.

Buying Skills: The Purchasing Agent's Opportunities

5

Buying Skills: The Purchasing Agent's Opportunities

"Scorn not the common man," says the age of abundance. "He may have no soul; his personality may be exactly the same as his neighbor's; and he may not produce anything worth having. But thank God, he consumes."

Joseph Wood Krutch, *"The Condition Called Prosperity,"* in Human Nature and Human Condition, 1959

As I mentioned at the beginning of this book, in a broad sense all negotiations occur in the context of getting (or buying) and giving (or selling). Variations in negotiating techniques result from variations in the value of the commodity, service, or favor being negotiated. What determines value? Certainly not money alone. Sometimes you can't even give money away on terms you deem

> The fact is, negotiations tend to be more complex when money is not an issue.

acceptable. Consider the recent example of the multi-millionaire who could not get the Metropolitan Museum in New York to accept a large sum to establish a communications school and center. Or the negotiation over whether New York should accept more than $1 billion from the federal government to build a highway on Manhattan's west side.

Buying and selling are not distinct and separate activities. Each should understand the other. They are opposite sides of the same coin. Many books have been written about selling but few about buying. Buying requires just as much skill, knowledge, and preparation. If buyers just look for the best value they can get for their or their companies' money, they are not doing the best job possible. Buyers should substitute negotiation for comparison shopping. That opens up creative alternatives upon which to base their decisions. The aim of negotiations can vary. For example, a buyer should consider that the seller's primary concern is to hold down production costs. Therefore, the buyer and seller should work together toward that result.

> To negotiate effectively, buyers and sellers must have equal, though sometimes different, skills.

You will have noted that I have chosen to use purchasing agents and salespeople to illustrate the techniques of buying and selling in the business world. This is not meant to imply that all corporate purchasing is channeled through a purchasing agent's office. We all know that it isn't. Purchases are also made by personnel departments when they use employment agencies, by financial departments when they employ outside accountants, and by sales departments when they seek the services of advertising agencies or buy advertising. All of these activities, and many more not mentioned, clearly demonstrate the kind of buy-and-sell negotiations that occur daily in the business world.

The Purchasing Agent's Job

But let's return to our example of the purchasing agent. The purchasing agent's job is to keep the company running by supplying needed goods and services at the right price. My investigations have revealed that most purchasing agents apparently don't have overall strategies or clearly articulated ultimate goals. This lack of direction is reinforced by their employers. Many corporations feel that procurement is merely an administrative function—that people other than purchasing managers determine what products to buy and that the purchasing agent's job is, therefore, rather hollow. Purchasing agents are the product of their experience. In other words, their actions are guided by past experience, good and bad.

Unfortunately, in most instances, experience tends to limit rather than broaden the scope of their activities. What makes the difference between a paper-pushing clerk and a functioning, skilled purchasing agent?

The Art of Negotiating®

When this art is effectively used, purchasing means knowing a company's internal structure, departmental functions, historical precedents, future plans, and long-range goals. Let's consider some internal responsibilities of purchasing agents, beginning with internal communication. On a horizontal level, purchasing agents should be in touch with other departments: engineering, sales, and so on. They should also extend communication vertically—up to management to give and receive information, and down to the employees in their departments to keep them informed and make the best use of their talents.

Vertically: Management should keep purchasing agents informed about their companies' operations and long- and short-term goals, so they can make purchasing decisions that best meet the needs of all departments and functions that might be affected by those decisions.

Horizontally: Purchasing agents should make it their business to find out about inventories, finances, scheduling, timing, and specifications. For example, purchasing agents' understanding of product specifications might permit them to suggest changes in designs, materials, and/or methods that would achieve substantial savings. Purchasing agents should also keep others within their companies informed about new products, possible substitutions regarding materials and/or methods, fluctuation costs, availability of materials, and new methods of production.

Purchasing agents should consider it part of their jobs to get management, other departments, and employees at their companies to accept the end products of their negotiations and go along with any internal changes that may be required to perform purchase contracts. Good purchasing agents communicate well with all personnel, from top management to clerical employees. They stay on top of developments in the industry and know as much as possible about available products that might improve their companies' efficiency and profitability.

> It is important to realize that purchasing agents learn from suppliers by negotiating.

Learning From Salespeople

Salespeople who feel they are being treated with respect for their knowledge and experience will serve their customers far better than those who feel they are considered a necessary evil. Negotiating also makes purchasing agents a focal point in relations between companies.

Purchasing agents should encourage the salespeople who come to them to present innovations, new products, and new uses for the agents' companies' products. Selling is really an educational process, and purchasers should take advantage of that process. Sellers can teach specifications, capabilities, and prices. Some companies attempt to make the most of this opportunity to learn from salespeople by requiring that purchasing agents buy from more than one company and/or by making suppliers bid against one another for important contracts.

When negotiating a transaction, many elements must be scrutinized by purchasing agents. For example, they might:

- Determine what variations on the basic technology are available.
- Study wages and hours data to determine which method of production is least costly.
- Find out the present state of development of a particular item.

- Determine the likelihood that a particular method of production might change in the near future.
- Find out whether all specifications are essential or if some could be modified to get a better price.
- Judge the reasonableness of the overhead in view of projected production.
- Study specifications or engineers' drawings of their own products to determine what information might benefit both buyer and seller.

Purchasing agents who have such information should not keep it to themselves, but should share it with sellers. They should let the sellers help formulate a better deal for both parties.

Analyzing Costs

One of the more direct ways for a purchasing agent to analyze the cost factor among competing products is to determine:

- the direct materials involved
- the direct labor involved
- the factory overhead
- administrative expenses

Purchasing agents don't have to be experts in each of these areas, but they should know how to get the data they need to make informed decisions. Sources of information include:

- The seller himself.
- The seller's competitors. It is helpful to research other, similar types of products or manufacturing processes.
- The purchasing agent's own buying organization, engineering department, and other staff departments.
- Published reports in any field concerning the project or product

Catching Common Errors

A thorough analysis of the various factors involved in any buying decision will help purchasing agents catch common errors. Such errors include:

- Inflated estimates of the future price.
- Prices based on a better grade of material than is necessary.
- Improper assessment of requirements.
- A small-quantity price for a large-quantity purchase.
- Wasteful disposal of scrap—an element of value that is too often neglected.

Labor costs. These can be broken down into two basic factors:

1. The number of hours
2. The hourly wage rate

Pricing and Negotiating

This may seem elementary, but prices often vary more widely than the basic cost of materials. It's important to remember that prices are not set in stone—people choose the ways and means by which prices are set. Prices are always subject to negotiation. It's also wise to act with the realization that to a substantial degree, pricing is based on inadequate information and just plain personal preference. Purchasing agents can use this in understanding pricing in their negotiations.

> The major objective of a purchasing agent's analysis should be to consider methods whereby both the purchaser and the seller can control costs and share the benefits.

Buyers can bring out many elements in negotiations. The very fact that price may be the result of administrative action based upon individual preference—without regard to demand, extent of competition, or competitive prices—can provide leverage in negotiations. A good negotiator might take the initiative by suggesting a rate of return that would be fair to both companies.

Possible Strategies

Strategies should not win a battle and lose the relationship. Knowledge of various strategies that sellers use to set prices will improve any purchasing agent's negotiating skills. Here's a list of different strategies. These are examples to demonstrate the strategies. They are not offered as manipulative tactics.

Forbearance: Sellers wait until the last possible moment to set their prices. After all, their competitors' prices already have been set.

Surprise: Sellers set unrealistic prices, more by hunch than by any logical system. Their intent is to make each and every buyer haggle over what his or her discount might be.

Fait Accompli: Sellers set price schedules, then wait to see buyers' reactions.

Bland Withdrawal: Sellers send out price lists and wait for some response. At the first sign of opposition, they back down and say, "No, that's not what we meant at all."

Apparent Withdrawal: If sellers' prices are criticized, they lead buyers to think that adjustments will be made, lulling them into a false sense of security. In the final analysis, they leave buyers without alternative sources, then keep the prices at the same levels that were first quoted.

Reversal: At the first sign of any pressure, sellers back down and give new quotations that tend to vary with the market. If sellers feel they can raise prices, they reverse themselves again.

Limits: Sellers contend that their policies have been successful for a number of years and that they will stick to their guns and hold prices to within certain prescribed limits.

Feinting: Sellers set up smokescreens to deceive purchasers into thinking that they are going to get something they're not. Sellers make buyers believe that they have all relevant information when, in fact, some important elements have been left out.

Participation: Sellers set their prices only after they have discussed it with the entire competition despite the fact that such price-fixing is, or may well be, illegal.

Association: Sellers get all their competitors' price lists, then make up their own lists. They then state that their prices are set by the competition.

Dissociation: Whatever price structure any of the competition uses, the sellers' will be different. They will not abide by any industry-wide standard practice. This can, in instances, lead to complete misunderstanding as to what their prices truly mean.

Crossroads: Sellers create tie-ins, bringing two or more elements of their price lists together. Their "best" prices are offered only when buyers meet all stipulated conditions.

Blanketing: Sellers' price lists supposedly cover such a wide area that when specific prices are quoted, it seems that the prices originally set forth were misleading.

Randomizing: Sellers who use this strategy are chartists who use advanced mathematics to set prices that may be far from realistic.

Random Sample: Sellers who sold at a certain profit ratio once may believe that established profit structure will last forever. If they change it, it is only to keep their profit margins in line with their costs.

Salami: Sellers cannot bring themselves to establish a set price. In their endeavor to keep prices variable, they will give each lot a separate price.

Bracketing: Sellers using this strategy set their prices above the mark, anticipating that buyers will offer prices below the mark. The sellers hope that they can split the difference.

The Purchasing Philosophy

Management should remember what John Ruskin once said:

> It is unwise to pay too much but it is worse to pay too little. When you pay too much you lose a little money. . . . When you pay too little, you sometimes lose everything, because the thing you bought was incapable of doing the thing it was bought to do. The common law of business balance prohibits paying a little and getting a lot—it can't be done. If you deal with the lowest bidder, it is well to add something for the risk you run. If you do that, you will have enough to pay for something better.

A final bit of purchasing philosophy comes from an anecdote told about astronaut Gordon Cooper, who, on returning from a space shot, was asked if he was ever worried. "Only once. While concentrating on the panel I suddenly looked at all the dials and gadgets and it occurred to me that every one of those parts was supplied by the lowest bidder."

Components of Buying/Selling Negotiation

How many purchasing agents you know are familiar with their stock in trade—the various forms of concessions they can make to get better prices and guarantees against price changes? Are they aware enough of the various payment terms that will allow them to get the proper discounts for cash, prepayments, quantity buying, and cumulative buying? Do they know what clauses will guarantee against both known and unknown possibilities? Are they aware of the long-term contract and when it would be useful to their organizations? Do they consider changes of specifications to meet the seller's needs that will not interfere with the type of product they are seeking? Is their timing right? Are they aware that seasonal buying may bring price reductions?

What are some of the elements that buyers and sellers should consider when evaluating the cost of making a profit? Buyers and sellers should look at:

- The input that is necessary for full performance.
- The management and technical effort necessary to acquire the materials and fulfill the contracts.
- The risks posed by the contract costs.
- The market. Is it rising or falling?
- The performance record of the other parties to contracts.
- The possibility that sellers are being asked to produce something unique or outside their usual fields, something that offers them little in the way of future orders or rewards.

If subsequent contracts are expected, and if they are to be much larger than the original orders, buyers might, as a matter of strategy, use the larger subsequent contracts as a "carrot" to get sellers to give lower prices on initial orders. This practice is known as *buying in.*

The purchasing agent who receives a seller's proposal should analyze that proposal by studying, for example, the history of the price involved, the various industrial and governmental indexes that are available, how the price was built up, how the price breaks down into its various elements, detailed cost estimates, contingency factors, value analysis, functional evaluation, and the vendor's cost analysis.

Buying and Selling Considerations

Certainly, both parties to a sale must take many factors into consideration *before* closing a deal. Let's take a look at some of them.

- Price, terms, and credit.
- Biases against some products (history or, experience).
- Can't reach a responsible party to make a deal.
- Competition unknown.
- Previous buying habits.
- Delivery-point, time, or manner.
- Consistency of product.
- Full services available and knowledge of parties' needs.
- Warranties offered.
- Bad reputation of source.
- Necessary specifications.
- Abilities of the supplier, such as technical competence.
- Availability of additional services, for example, engineering, repairs, financial data, and so forth.
- Developing a new source.
- Relations or friends benefited by purchase.
- A possible offset against other purchases from supplier.
- Funds available in fiscal year.
- Timing of the purchase (seasonal).
- Inventory—both buyer's and supplier's.
- Following what your competition is doing.
- Inflation or deflation trend.

- Buying into and holding a source—eliminating competition.
- National origin of a source (may be important).
- Breaking into a market for the product.

Strategies For Buyers

Several strategies are available to purchasers to get the prices they are willing to pay for items or services. They might say that the base price is not the sole determinant of who will get the order.

They might wish to:

- Emphasize terms.
- Get the supplier to work with them to meet their overall goals.
- Get a group price, then pick one item for purchase from that group (cherry picking).
- Point out that it is not the money but the total benefits that interest their firms.
- Insist on such things as service, warranties, quality, delivery, ability, reliability, peace of mind, and reputation.
- Indicate that any price change should warrant other concessions.

Contents of Price Discussions

Before entering into a discussion of prices, one should be aware of the many options. Most price discussions should include a review of:

- All available alternatives: design, terms, group price, package deal, tie-in, delivery, quality, quantity, and whether or not the seller will be the sole supplier.
- The potential for split product and services, that is, letting the buyer perform some parts, tasks, or steps to save time, money, or both.

- The wide variety of payment plans available—what payment arrangement would best fulfill the needs of both parties.

- The potential for dividing the risk-taking, thus sharing unknown or unforeseen losses.

- Guarantees and grievance procedures to reduce risk and resolve disputes.

- The type of negotiation—price, cost-plus, or individual items.

- Any other possible options that may be available.

- Opportunities to buy into future business.

- Each item that makes up the total cost—a destructive analysis.

- Past rule-of-thumb estimates.

- Benefits of quantity purchases.

- Who gets what regarding scrap and spoilage.

- Possible incentive pricing.

- Terms to redetermine price under specified circumstances.

- What benefits can be enjoyed if the purchaser takes the entire production run (or capacity) of the seller.

- What technical assistance—and how much—the seller will provide.

Cost vs. Price Contracts

Much can be learned by comparing negotiations for a cost contract with negotiations for a total price contract. A price contract is negotiated strictly on the basis of price—the final figure that the buyer has to pay. Cost contracts, on the other hand, take into consideration all the costs involved in producing an item. A reasonable profit is then added to produce the amount agreed upon under the contract.

If an impasse is reached in negotiating a price contract, a cost contract may be an alternative that offers advantages to both buyer and seller. The advantages to be derived from cost negotiation are:

- It requires that buyers prepare more effectively and in greater detail.

- It requires that sellers examine each factor that has gone into each calculation and prevents them from padding costs or misapplying certain costs.

- Finally, when both parties have made detailed cost analyses, it makes them more likely to make their own improvements to take advantage of savings that can be gained from reducing technical requirements or using different materials.

Of course, sellers can ask for a contingency allowance on each cost element. A seller can subdivide a contract so each element of the item produced becomes a separate contract segment with a separate price for each. Such separate agreements have a tendency to enlarge seller profits. When contingency allowances are written into contracts, buyers should realize that the whole probably will not equal the sum of the parts. At least some of the contingencies will arise, so the corresponding allowances will be charged. In its dealings with defense contractors, the U.S. government has found many times that the whole can be greater than the sum of its parts. For this reason the amount under a price contract can be lower than that under a cost contract.

> With a knowledge of the sellers' needs, buyers can offer creative alternatives that will benefit both buyer and seller.

Buyers who negotiate creatively can minimize this drawback to cost contracts in a number of ways. For example, they can reexamine their assumptions and possibly find that less stringent specifications are possible on certain items, thus lowering the cost. They can suggest broader marketing possibilities for certain items, which might also lower costs.

They can suggest alternate suppliers for items that are produced more efficiently elsewhere.

Getting a Price Breakdown

These are also explained, not recommended if manipulative tactics might injure a relationship. If you are a purchaser, you might want your suppliers to provide you with price breakdowns. Such a request is sheer logic—from your standpoint. After all, it's part of your job to ensure that your company gets a fair price. Nonetheless, you may encounter resistance from some or all of your suppliers. If so, break down that resistance by telling suppliers:

- It is our legal requirement to have one.
- Your competition is providing price breakdowns.
- I may have to go over your head, to a higher authority, to secure the price breakdown I am requesting.
- I will make it worth your while by giving you additional business once you provide the breakdown.
- I cannot make a purchasing decision (limited authority) without it.
- I need it to check your analysis.

When the Shoe's on the Other Foot: If, on the other hand, you are the seller, you may have a number of reasons for not wanting to provide a breakdown showing how you arrived at the quoted price. To avoid providing such information, you might:

- Agree to provide the breakdown but drag your feet, causing delays.
- Provide only partial information or your "best estimate."
- Provide information that is excessively detailed.
- Agree to the request, but caution that a fee will be charged for doing so.
- Inform the purchaser that trade secrets or proprietary information is involved.

- Provide the requested information but bury it among other information and tell the purchaser that it cannot be separated out.

You can see that many moves can occur in a cost negotiation, but the end result should be that as much information as possible is shared and things are worked out to everyone's advantage. When both sides have the information they need to make a penetrating analysis of all elements of a transaction, they arrive at creative alternatives that can lead to improvements in terms of altered materials, revised buying practices, relaxed specifications, simplified manufacturing processes, and so forth. This is "pie-expanding negotiation."

Key Points

Purchasing agents should work as hard as salespeople to achieve an Everybody Wins® conclusion. Their knowledge and use of The Art of Negotiating®, their ability to deal on every level, their ability to learn from all and to analyze costs, and their knowledge of pricing will help guarantee their continued success.

Above all, they should understand and adopt a purchasing philosophy based on value—not price only—that will enable them to develop and maintain relationships that are profitable to both themselves and those they buy from.

Selling: The Reverse Side of the Coin

Selling: The Reverse Side of the Coin

"Everything is worth what its purchaser will pay for it."

Publilius Syrus, Moral Sayings, (1st century B.C.)

Now we come to selling, the other side of the same coin. As was shown, salespeople should know as much as possible about a buyer's needs and problems, and how the seller's product can meet them. *This knowledge can close sales even before prices are quoted.*

As a salesperson, analyzing what you are selling is a substantial part of your job. Self-analysis in this area is vital. If your selling concept coincides with the buyer's objectives, the sale may be made long before you quote prices or start writing up orders. During the initial stage of negotiations, take time to compare your concepts with the buyer's objectives. Then you can work on bringing all sides together.

Getting to the Decision Maker

A seller should know who makes the decisions at the purchasing company. Decisions are not necessarily made by the person who has the title and responsibility. Decisions might be made by the chairman of the board's secretary! If that's the case, the salespeople had better reevaluate their strategies and tactics accordingly, to meet the acid situation. In addition to the decision makers themselves, a seller should get to know all who have an influence on the customer's buying decisions. Many times, sellers can establish an alliance with these key people. If sellers take the time to conduct in-depth analyses,of the purchasers' operations, they will uncover important relationships and will avoid stepping on anybody's toes within a buyer's firm.

Salespeople also should enlist the cooperation of people within their own firms, thus enabling them to offer their customers every available resource connected with the product being purchased. Buyers know that price is only one component of value—and not necessarily the most important.

> Too many salespeople fail to make purchasers aware of the resources of the organizations they represent.

Salespeople are representatives of their companies. They must be able to convince buyers that they can marshal all of their companies' resources to fulfill buyer needs. Whether a company is large or small, its salespeople should make it clear to buyers that the company can get the job done—that sales is really an arm or branch of the entire organization, and that the sales staff can marshal the seller's full resources on the buyers' behalf.

Several Union Carbide salespeople met with their supervisors to discuss an upcoming negotiation. They were told how to demonstrate that the full resources of the entire organization were at the customer's disposal, not how to handle issues of price. The sales supervisors knew from previous experience that this was more important, both to Union Carbide and to its customers, than questions concerning price.

Strategies to Determine the Price That Your Competition is Offering

Understand that you can do much to avoid price being a stumbling block to your sales negotiations. For instance, antitrust laws state that suppliers to large companies must offer the same prices to all buyers of the same item, but they can adjust their charges to meet competitive prices. How can a salesperson find out what has been offered by the competition? Here are different approaches to get the answer without asking the question.

- **Forbearance:** "You know I can't do much about the price unless you tell me what my competition is doing."
- **Surprise:** Misstate. "You're paying $1.45 a pound now. . . . No? Oh, you're paying $1.43."
- *Fait accompli:* "Your competitor just gave us a large order at $1.45."
- **Bland withdrawal:** "Take their offer of $1.40."
- **Apparent withdrawal:** "I don't believe we could afford to meet their price, let alone beat it."
- **Reversal:** "You suggest a fair price, and I'll meet it."
- **Limits:** "We both know what the price is today, but would you care to be committed to what it's going to be three months from now?"
- **Feinting:** "I'd offer it to you at $1.43, but only if I were sure that's what you're buying it for."
- **Participation:** "We've had a good business relationship for a long time, so I want to give you the best price I legally can."
- **Association:** "Our product meets the highest standards in the industry, but we want to be competitive."
- **Dissociation:** "Their price is probably right, but could you be sure of getting the same high quality?"
- **Crossroads:** "You have to consider other things besides price: delivery date, dependability of supply, and quality control. What was the best package they could offer?"

- **Blanketing:** "The market has been very volatile lately. Everyone seems to be shifting on price. What's the best offer you've received?"

- **Randomizing:** "I'll toss you for your order."

- **Random Sample:** "Most of our competition would offer it to you at $1.45 without understanding your special needs, but I'm not sure we would be able to if we did that."

- **Salami:** "We could probably shave a point here and there to get to a competitive price."

- **Bracketing:** "You know the market too well to pay $1.50 a pound, and I know that nobody could be selling it to you for as little as $1.30. But if I quote you $1.45, and you're now paying $1.45, that wouldn't do me any good. . . ." (and so on, until the correct figure is met).

- **Changing Levels:** "The industry as a whole would charge you $1.45, but we're interested in what Jim Baldwin at XYZ Company is offering, and we'll meet his price."

Not all sellers have the same problems. If a company is a giant in a particular field, special rules apply. When a firm is dominant in the field, it is concerned about antitrust laws. A giant is permitted under the law to meet a competitive price but not to beat it. If a customer tells a large company that it is buying a product at $10\frac{1}{2}$ cents, the large company is allowed to meet the $10\frac{1}{2}$ cent price. It cannot offer $10\frac{1}{2}$ cents. And if the customer misleads the selling company by saying it is getting the product for 10 cents, when in reality it is paying $10\frac{1}{2}$ cents, then the customer is guilty of an antitrust violation.

The following tactics again are only for education Any use should avoid manipulation. They were used by some salespeople of a dominant chemical manufacturer to find out what price its customers were getting from the competition.

Bracketing: When this chemical company's salespeople see customers, they usually don't ask directly, "What price are you paying?" Instead, they go to the customers and say, "I know that you're too experienced to pay eleven cents a pound, and I know you couldn't buy it for ten cents." Now the sales representatives are bracketed in. They know the area. "If I wanted to offer it to you at ten and three fourths, it would do me no good if you were paying ten and a fourth." By bracketing, the sales reps have zeroed in on the target. They know pretty well where the prices fall. They can keep probing in this way by asking a series of questions. The sales reps get the customers to disclose prices without committing themselves.

Candid approach: A second way for salespeople to handle the situation is by saying to their customers, "Look, if you make me guess what price your other suppliers are giving you, and I meet that price—let's say ten and a half cents—without absolutely knowing that that's what you're paying, the antitrust laws say I must offer the same price to all your competitors. However, if you tell me what your price is, and I can meet it, then I don't have to offer that price to your competitors. For example, if you tell me that your price is, say, ten and a half cents, I can meet that price for this transaction only. I don't have to offer the same price to your competitors." This approach takes advantage of the fact that if a seller lowers the price just to meet the competition, it does not have to offer the same reduced price to all its other customers.

Feinting: In this situation, the salespeople say, "With your price in mind we can make the regular quantities available. . . ." The sellers draw the buyers into conversations without any mention of price. The salespeople speak in such a manner that the buyers become convinced that the salespeople know the prices they pay and have taken those figures for granted. Then, in the course of the conversations, the buyers may mention prices or divulge other information that enables the sellers to deduce what prices the buyers are paying.

Misstatement: A fourth way to find out what buyers are already paying works like this: "I know that you're paying twelve and a half cents. . . ." The buyer interrupts, "What do you mean twelve and a half cents? I'm only paying ten and a half." The salespeople then come back with "I meant ten and a half. Sorry." Intentional misstatements have produced the necessary information. Or the misstatement might be, "I hear the price has gone up." To which the buyers might reply, "No, no, the price is still the same. . . ."

Opinions: A fifth way of getting price information is to ask buyers' opinions: "Look, I respect your ability to analyze the market. Now, what do you think the market for the product is today?"

You are not asking the buyers how much they pay, you are asking for their evaluation of marketing conditions. Usually, you will get straightforward answers using this tactic, provided you have established a relationship characterized by mutual respect.

Price Alone May Be Unimportant

A salesperson who realizes that price as a single item is unimportant is well on the way to success. Certainly, price is one element of value, but the product must fit into an entire process. The full-scale relationship of a particular product to a process, not the dollar cost alone, represents the value. Every element of the process is of equal importance. If any element does not stand up, the entire process will probably fail.

Salespeople should learn about the values they represent, that is, their own companies' objectives and products and the present and future business potential of their own and the purchasers' companies. Salespeople must be interested in their customers' ability to continue in business and improve profits, and they must also demonstrate that they can help customers meet objectives. These factors are vital to establishing relationships with buyers.

A Buying and Selling Checklist

Let's assume you are about to enter into a negotiation that presumably will result in a buy/sell agreement. It doesn't matter whether you are the buyer or the seller. Here is a

> Remember, buying and selling are opposite sides of the same coin, and both can follow the same "script."

checklist equally suitable to either the buyer or the seller:

- Are you aware of when your negotiation starts?
- What preparations do you routinely make before arriving at this point?
- Have you separated areas of initial agreement from issues to be negotiated?
- Because areas of agreement are determined in large part by mutual assumptions, have you carefully examined your basis for assumptions to be sure they will hold up?
- Do you objectively feel you can change your opposer's attitude while your own remains unchanged?
- Will you make an effort to create a negotiating climate? How will it be effective? (See Chapter Eleven.)
- Are you prepared to listen actively? (See page 37.)
- Have you prepared a question map in advance? (See page 43.)
- Will you allow sufficient time for the questions to be answered fully?
- Will you be able to change your mind-set regarding the one "right" way to handle an issue if the other party offers alternatives?
- Will you understand and make an effort to overcome semantic difficulties and technical language?
- Do you know when and how to use disclosure and the risks involved? (See Chapter Nine.)

- Are you prepared to draw a clear distinction between initial fact finding and subsequent negotiating?
- Do you impose limits too quickly?
- Do you close doors to alternatives or do you welcome them?
- Do you know how to use concessions effectively in negotiations? (Answers to these questions are given throughout the book.)

Sellers have to show potential buyers that they provide better value (perhaps because their products mean less work), have added promotional value, allow for greater profitability, or provide growth opportunities.

The sellers' products also might represent consolidation of supply or additional sources of supply, either of which can be a selling point. If sellers negotiating with a previous customer give better service than the competition, past performance may be remembered and rewarded. Sellers might point out that their companies are not in competition with the buyers and will not enter into competition. They might show how purchasing their products will help the buyers break into a market or firm up an existing market. Sellers should evaluate tax advantages, credit advantages, research and development advantages, and information advantages to their customers. They should review the buyer's every possible need, then try to envision how they can fill those needs.

> In the overall scheme, buyers and sellers have the same objectives, but it's up to the sellers to lay the groundwork for satisfactory arrangements to achieve those objectives.

Dos and Don'ts for Creating Positive Selling Climates

Don't

- Use gestures and phrases that are inconsistent with what is being said. For example, speakers should not say, "I would never lie to you," when no one has accused them of lying.
- Automatically depend on strategies and tactics that have worked before.
- Use an unlimited number of questions. They create anxieties.
- Allow for interruptions or contradictions.
- Use technical terms, jargon, or cliches without clarifying them.
- Use voice tones that are emotional or abrasive.
- Employ value judgments.
- Give your opponent either/or alternatives.

Do

- Use language and gestures that are appropriate to the climate you intend to create.
- Be open-minded to all potential strategies and tactics.
- Use questions to establish needs, clarify issues, guide the discussion, and consider new alternatives.
- Listen carefully, and evaluate carefully.
- Utilize clear, direct, to-the-point communication.
- Use voice tones that are calm and matter-of-fact.
- Use neutral terms, free of value judgments.
- Consider all suitable alternatives.

Climate Control

There is no one method or climate that is "best" in all instances, certainly not in buying-selling negotiations.

Salespeople must use their imaginations to sell their products. In the process, they may have to sell the buyers on different methods of buying. Salespeople must always be ready to sell their customers on the idea of changing the way they buy. As an illustration: Some companies have decided that they get the best terms by requiring sellers to submit bids. But while competitive bidding can be valuable, it does have certain disadvantages.

Many large firms do not favor submitting bids. They find themselves at a disadvantage compared with smaller companies. Smaller firms can make decisions more rapidly, make adjustments to their bids, and more often succeed in getting the orders by competitive bidding.

A salesman for a large firm found the following method useful in overcoming the bidding problem: He tried to change the bidding situation into a negotiating situation. This was done by submitting, in answer to the request for a bid, prices or terms that were somewhat ambiguous and indefinite. For example, if the delivery term was to be six months, the bid would specify delivery in not less than six months. The buyer would then have to call the salesman to ask about the vague term. At that time the salesman would be in a position to initiate negotiations. He would be in a position to point out that the bidding method cannot take into account subsequent charging market conditions and that a negotiated price for shorter terms than even six months with price protection might better serve the interests of the buying company.

Key Points

No matter whether you are a buyer or a seller, knowing and acquiring the skills of both is essential to success in the purchasing/selling process. You can follow the lists of Dos and Don'ts, the checklists, or the suggested approaches. Or you can use them as guides to stimulate your thinking and come up with your own new, creative alternatives.

Negotiating Skills For Real Estate: Making the Big Sale

7

Negotiating Skills For Real Estate: Making the Big Sale

"How often have I said to you that when you have eliminated the impossible, whatever remains, however improbable, must be true."

Sir Arthur Conan Doyle, *"The Sign of Four"*

Sooner or later, many of us will be involved in some kind of real estate transaction. As a first step, it's important to analyze the difference between why the seller wants to sell and why the buyer wants to buy. Obviously, the parties view the property differently: The buyer sees the property in an entirely different light than the seller. Perhaps the buyer feels he or she is a little more creative or better informed than the seller.

On Lying and Half-Truths: Here, as in other purchasing transactions, there is grave danger to your self in asking the seller why he or she is selling. The danger is that you are likely to believe the seller, and therefore not investigate the proposition as thoroughly as you should. The seller will give excellent reasons why he or she is selling a piece of property, while, without skipping a beat, expounding on the property's growth potential and declaring that the property is the finest piece of land anyone could possibly own

For example, the seller might open up a desk drawer and pull out an electrocardiogram showing that he or she has a

0

heart condition and must give up all work. In other words, the seller was prepared for that question and, instead of the truth, will give an answer that he or she feels will somehow induce you to buy.

Lying seldom benefits the liar over the long haul. In the words of William Shakespeare, "Truth will come to light." For that reason, it's essential to find out as much as possible about the opposing parties themselves and about the

> Nonetheless, it behooves an expert negotiator to understand that some shortsighted parties, who can't see beyond "closing the deal," will use lies or half-truths to overcome objections.

property involved. Independent investigation is the key. Be wary of representations by an opposing party that aren't corroborated by your information.

Brokers: A Vital Function

Few people know how to use brokers in real estate transactions. Brokers serve a vital function. They are your antennae. They're out in the field, feeding you information regarding sources of financing, areas for development, and methods of closing transactions.

All of these are vital to any real estate transaction. However, there are also certain areas where you don't want your broker involved. For example, a broker might believe that part of his or her duty is to negotiate for you. That should rarely be the case. An opportune time for using a broker in this way is when you want an agent with limited authority. When you do not want to commit yourself to any final decision, it can be useful to have the broker submit and receive propositions. Because there's no necessity of a face-to-face meeting between you and the other party, there's no risk that you might have to make or break a deal on the basis of an offer. You always get a second chance to go in as a principal and vary the terms.

There are inherent limitations with the use of an agent. The agent, broker, or attorney, as the case may be, won't want you to develop fixed expectations until the position of the other side becomes clear. The agent will try to prevent you from freezing your position early. If you freeze, he or she will try to alter your point of view, usually by getting or revealing new information. For example, the agent might say he or she can get the property for you at a cheaper price.

An agent usually doesn't get his or her commission until the closing. Therefore, when the preliminary contract is signed, there is a possibility that some agent will do his or her best to make you feel that the deal meets your needs and expectations. For example, he or she will say, "You have everything you need."

In many cases, an agent may not reveal all aspects of a contract unless you, the principal, insist on knowing all details of the proposed transaction. The agent may blithely assume that everything will turn out all right. He or she rationalizes the withholding of information, theorizing that the circumstances you are worried about rarely happen.

Key Points

Whenever there is a third party involved—broker, lawyer, mortgage provider, or others—use all of your negotiating skills to understand as much as possible about just what is happening. Don't just rely on reports of the third party. Many want to play the role of the hero in settling a negotiation.

Strategies and Counterstrategies

Strategies and Counter-strategies

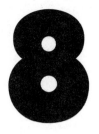

"Seek not proud riches, but such as thou mayest get justly, use soberly, distribute cheerfully, and leave contentedly."

Francis Bacon, "Of Riches," Essays, 1625

Negotiating strategies and counterstrategies are essential tools in changing relationships, the goal of any negotiation. They are, however, only one element of the negotiating process. All too often, buyers and sellers alike needlessly confine themselves to a limited repertoire. They regard negotiating as a game where, if they are lucky, they will "win." All of their needs will be met, and all of their desires will be satisfied. When this does not happen, they look for strategic "tricks" that will surely work.

The master negotiator recognizes that strategies are merely tools that can be used by the amateur and the artist alike, that only an end result where everybody wins can be considered an artistic triumph.

When the stakes are high and someone wins big, you may be sure that the losers will all be sore and out for blood. The success of greenmail, a form of legal extortion, is a case in point. The "winner" buys a large block of stocks in a major corporation, then sells them to the corporation at a much higher price than he paid. Score: one happy winner, thousands of irate stockholders whose holdings are valued at a lower price than the winner got, and one punch-drunk corporation. Walt Disney Productions was a victim of this unedifying strategy.

To wash the bad taste of the Disney affair out of your mouth you might consider the sales strategy of Dr. Robert I. Schattner, a chemist and dentist, who invented Chloraseptic (sodium phenolate). In 1952 while at a party he was asked why dentists had nothing to relieve soreness after a tooth extraction. He went to work on the problem, concentrating on phenol, which he had used to desensitize teeth and to treat mouth sores. He made phenol safer to use by buffering it, creating sodium phenolate, which is not toxic to oral tissues. He had it tested successfully and won FDA approval for Chloraseptic to be sold over the counter.

Now "all" Schattner needed to do was to sell it. He had no sales force so, adopting bracketing as a sales strategy, he aimed first at dentists in his neighborhood, distributing free samples to them. They used them up and wanted more. He aimed at local druggists, gave them free samples and told the dentists where they could buy new supplies. When the druggists ran out, he gave Chloraseptic to a wholesaler and told the druggists where they could buy it. Using "common sense," as he said, he told the wholesalers they would have to pay for the product only when—and if—they reordered it. Thus, he hit the target he was actually aiming at. He used the same strategy in developing an ever-expanding market. His payoff? In 1963 he sold his company, Norwich Pharmaceutical Co., for $4 million plus continuing royalties. Did anyone lose? Apparently not. The brand was later taken over by Procter & Gamble. When last heard from, Dr. Schattner had a new company, Sporicidin Co., and a new product that promised to cut the cost of supplying, operating, and sterilizing kidney dialysis machines by many millions of dollars a year.

Helping the Blind to See

In June 1984 a legally blind photographer, George Covington, conducted a six-hour workshop, at the National Portrait Gallery. Sponsored by the Smithsonian Institution and the Polaroid Corp., it featured demonstrations of camera equipment, photographic equipment, and film developing designed especially for the legally blind. Covington said, "Other people see to photograph. I photograph to see." His technique allows the photographer to compensate for a particular sight problem by adjusting light, size, and distance. Through photography, the legally blind can see objects they had not been able to see in person.

Frequently, when you're studying an all-embracing subject such as negotiating, you become blinded to alternatives in your field because you've "always done it" a certain way. It is then time to adjust your perspective and be able to see the subject in a new light.

Selling and Diplomacy

Recently, an opportunity arose to take a step-by-step look at opposing points of view of high-level diplomatic negotiations. There can be a number of insights into high-level sales to be gained from the study. Compare selling approaches with the diplomatic ways. Tom Paine wrote in 1791: "A diplomatic character is the narrowest sphere of society that man can act in. It forbids intercourse by a reciprocity of suspicion, and a diplomatist is a sort of unconnected atom, continually repelling and repelled." Is there any reason to change this definition even after 192 years?

A prize example of the concept of negotiation by negation can be found in the *New York Times*, January 16, 1983. In a follow-up story on the dismissal of Eugene V. Rostow, director of the U.S. Arms Control and Disarmament Agency, the *Times* reported that U.S. and Soviet negotiators had worked out an informal agreement limiting deployment of medium-range missiles in Europe.

Dismayed by Rostow's attempt to move the interminable talks off dead center, the Reagan Administration fired Rostow. The reason? He had exceeded his authority. Even more serious, a "senior State Department official" said, was that "a mythology may be created in Europe by all this that Rostow and Nitze negotiated a breakthrough that Neanderthals in Washington blocked."

In negotiation by negation, you see, appearance is everything—substance is nothing. In our broadened approach to negotiating, this breakthrough would have been considered an opening wedge, to be further widened.

In an effort to clarify some major differences between two competing philosophies of negotiation—negotiation by negation, where one side wins everything and the other loses all, and creative negotiation, where both sides win—it may be instructive to consider a type of negotiation to which very few of you would ever be a party. Contrast Yehezkel Dror "21 Rules for Negotiating Rulers" (*The Jerusalem Quarterly*, Number 25, Fall 1982) with The Art of Negotiating® techniques.

Noting the importance of face-to-face negotiations by heads of government, Dror, a teacher of political science at the Hebrew University, Jerusalem, nevertheless warns of the grave dangers inherent in giving rulers the power to conduct important bargaining and negotiations "at will." To counteract this perceived danger he offers his 21 rules. The headings describing the rules are listed below, each followed by our counter-suggestions. Can the diplomatic rules limitations be helpful in recognizing sales/buying limitations?

Rule One:
Beware of Personal Negotiations

Counter: Up close and face-to-face negotiation has the advantage of preventing miscalculation and of instantly clarifying ambiguities. It allows for more intimate experiences. It also expedites the negotiation process as no mere agent with limited authority can. If you fear being cornered, prepare in advance for a graceful retirement. No ruler would rule long if he or she were forced to spend months and years dickering in a foreign land. That role is relegated to an agent who can be and often is repudiated.

> Don't fear personal negotiations.
> Understand in advance the advantages and disadvantages, and prepare for them.

Rule Two:
Don't Trust Blind Intuition

Counter: Blind intuition is not a negotiating tool. It is the use of animal cunning to spot a weakness in an opposer that will result in his or her defeat. However, developed intuition, founded on wisdom and experience, can discover the opposer's real needs and suggest ways to satisfy them, thus paving the way for agreement.

Rule Three:
Base Tragic Choices on Long-Range Considerations

Counter: This is the rationalization for the statement, "The end justifies the means." Rather than be satisfied with this rationale, a fuller assessment of the situations, present and long-range, must be made. This will take the form of using your creative talents and not being satisfied until choices present themselves that are consistent with your important values, beliefs, commitments, and goals.

Rule Four:
Interact Closely with Your Staff

Counter: No man is an island, no matter how powerful he may be. Neither is a ruler and his staff of subordinates. Reliance on any single point of view, whether your own or your

> Interact with every participant in a negotiation.

staff's, can be blinding. You may find yourself isolated and without agreement.

Rule Five:
Be Creative, with Self-Doubt

Counter: Do not impose artificial limits such as self-doubts on your creativity. Test your creative thinking by changing levels and/or points of view, but do not be afraid of thinking the "unthinkable." Every creative thought you have is, for you at least, a leap into the unknown. Experience is creative thinking lighting the way.

Rule Six:
Go After Real Impact, Not Legal Formulations

Counter: Understand that the "real" world lies behind the symbolic words we use to deal with the real world. "Harsh reality" can only be experienced through the filters of our senses. Dror elaborates on Rule Six: "The test of an agreement and of the negotiation process, as a whole, is in their real impact on harsh reality, not in any covenant of words." Theobald (van) Bethmann Hollweg put it another way " . . . just for a scrap of paper, Great Britain is going to make war." The experienced negotiator would add, "and someone is going to end up the loser." The Book of Genesis, on the other hand, describes the real negotiating aim of any wise ruler: "I will establish my covenant between me and thee and thy seed after thee . . . ."

Rule Seven:
Consider Explicitly the Costs and Benefits of Ambiguity

Counter: Ambiguity is just another negotiating strategy. As such it is neither "good" nor "bad," *per se*. If you want to rely on it, help and hope that the circumstances will become beneficial to

> All strategies must be evaluated for potential benefits and possible roadblocks.

you. Otherwise, your use of ambiguity may result, as Dror warns, in planting "a time-bomb certain to blow up in your face at the wrong time." You then have *prima-facie* evidence that you have misused the strategy.

Rule Eight:
Regard Agreement as Just a Link in a Chain

Counter: In a win-or-lose negotiation, an agreement is meant to be a chain for the loser and a leash for the winner to hold. In an Everybody Wins® negotiation it is a bond between allies which time will possibly strengthen. Make sure as you end each negotiation that you have laid the foundation for future beneficial relations and agreements.

Rule Nine:
Study Your Partner Carefully and Act Accordingly

Counter: "Know thyself" is equally important. Everyone is different. A successful negotiation depends on the ability of both sides to deal with those differences.

Rule Ten:
Plan Your "Spontaneity"

Counter: Planned spontaneity is essential to low comedy and utterly inappropriate to serious negotiation. Don't put on acts. Most people see through them.

> Present a plan as well thought out, and a spontaneous thought for what it is—a creative attempt to move the negotiation forward.

Rule Eleven:
Willingly Exchange Symbols for Concrete Achievements

Counter: "A decent respect for the opinions of mankind" can and should be a primary goal for a competent negotiator. One thing is worth noting about Thomas Jefferson, whose words were just quoted. Late in life he requested that only this appear on his tombstone:

Here was buried
Thomas Jefferson
Author of the Declaration of American
Indepedance [his spelling]
of the Statute of Virginia for religious freedom
& Father of the University of Virginia

Those who believe pomp, circumstance, and symbols of power are the things that make life worth living may wonder: Where is mention of Jefferson's being Governor of Virginia? President of the United States? Initiator of the Louisiana Purchase? The other achievements of this extraordinary man?

I like to believe that Jefferson thought only those three achievements were worthy of mention because they were the products of hard and honest negotiation that benefited and honored not only his opposers of the moment but present and future generations.

Rule Twelve:
Select Negotiating Strategies Rationally

Counter: In elaborating on this rule, Dror mentions these strategies: "a choice bag of surprise offers, a stubborn or amenable posture, image of spontaneity or circumspections . . . and others."

> It is necessary to ask: Is it rational to tailor your strategies only to your perceived needs? Create a positive climate and conclusion. That should determine your strategies.

Rule Thirteen:
Orchestrate the Negotiation Context

Counter: Proper preparation will enable a negotiator to stay in close contact with changing realities, which many times during the negotiation are outside the orchestrated context.

Rule Fourteen:
Recognize and Face Uncertainties

Dror explains: ". . . all important decisions are in essence fuzzy bets, a kind of lottery whose rules are unclear and constantly shifting."

Counter: If you regard negotiation as a win-or-lose game, then the winner is entitled to say the rules are what he says they are. It is better to get on higher (and firmer) ground. If both sides emerge as winners, the rules are quite clear: The needs of both parties must be considered and the satisfaction of those needs must be maximized, no matter how uncertain life is.

Rule Fifteen:
Be Prepared for Failure

Counter: Do not rely on fall-back positions. Instead, always have alternative solutions for your major problem, the mutual satisfaction of needs. Mastery in reading nonverbal communications and other signals of the

> If you insist that every negotiation must have a winner and a loser, then, of course, you also must accept the fact that sooner or later you will be "it."

opposer will tell you when to try a new approach.

Rule Sixteen:
Remember Human Engineering

Counter: Preparation for negotiation includes full personal mental and physical preparation. Be the first to recognize your areas of potential weakness and expose your opposers if they try to interfere with or deny you satisfaction of your most basic needs. Do not allow hostile climates to go unrecognized. Respond to a negative climate positively, for the benefit of all. Go beyond the mechanistic "human engineering" approach.

Rule Seventeen:
Base Agreement on Real Complementary Interests

Counter: The Nierenberg Need Theory of Negotiating helps you identify the needs that can motivate both you and your opposer. An almost infinite number of ways to satisfy those needs provides the "shared real interest" that brought the negotiation about in the first place.

Rule Eighteen:
Cultivate Domestic Support

Counter: Control and cultivate are related here. Why attempt to manipulate public opinion? Negotiate for support based upon the perceived needs of yourself and your nation. This is an essential preparation for negotiation summitry

Rule Nineteen:
Invest In Your Staff

Counter: Acquire competent people. Create a positive working climate by recognizing their needs as well as your own Still, beware of reliance upon any single point of view. Relying only upon the views of their staffs has been a fault of several U.S. presidents.

> When you think you have the "only" or "best" way, your mind stops working.

Rule Twenty:
Don't Despise Formalized Methodologies

Counter: Understand all methodologies, old and new, that may help you negotiate creatively, but recognize that there is no such thing as "the only."

Rule Twenty-One:
Accept Historic Responsibility

Counter: Do not "play" so that you alone win. History will treat you much more kindly if you negotiate so that everyone wins.

Different Views for Diplomats at Different Times

As Machiavelli wrote for the "Prince" of his day, Dror's attempt to apply Machiavellian strategies to modern-day diplomatic needs seems downright constructive, compared to a new strategy much employed today. *Confrontational diplomacy* has replaced traditional methods, which Caskie Stinnett described: "A diplomat is a person who can tell you to go to hell in such a way that you actually look forward to the trip."

A few years ago, before the Gulf War, a U.S. delegate to the United Nations told the entire Assembly, "Begone!" Diplomatic nicety apparently prevented him from adding Oliver Cromwell's words to the Rump Parliament, "It is not fit that you sit here any longer!" Instead, he promised to see them off, waving as they "sailed into the sunset." Some wondered if it was malice aforethought or ignorance that led him to urge the delegates from the "morass" of the United Nations westward into the swamps of New Jersey, but seasoned observers dismissed it as another skirmish between "right-thinking Americans" and the "striped-pants diplomats." Still others noted with a certain bemusement that the incident took place shortly after the 200th anniversary of the signing of the Treaty of Paris (September 3, 1783).

How different diplomacy was then! Today, the treaty is remembered in the United States (if at all) as the formal recognition by Great Britain of U.S. independence. It was, however, also a large-scale peace settlement among the warring European powers: Great Britain against France and Spain and against the Dutch as "armed neutrals." (Austria, with the encouragement of France, also played a meddlesome and ultimately unsuccessful role in the peacemaking process.)

An All-star Cast

The Anglo-American settlement has rightly been termed "the greatest triumph in the history of American diplomacy." And no wonder! The chief U.S. plenipotentiaries were Benjamin Franklin, who as minister to France had helped gain French recognition (and financial and military help) for the new nation, John Adams, later President of the United States, who had already negotiated the adoption of the Declaration of Independence by the Second Continental Congress and, having some free time, drafted the Constitution of Massachusetts, still in effect today (although with many amendments), and negotiated U.S. recognition by the Dutch government (and a much-needed loan); and, finally, John Jay, later first Chief Justice of the United States, who had served as minister plenipotentiary to Spain (and negotiated a loan), among many other services.

The adventures of these American diplomats during months of tortuous negotiations with the great powers have filled many books. As for the U.N. diplomat whose "only" solution to a problem was to order his opposers out of the country, *The Peace-Makers*, by Richard B. Morris (Harper & Row, 1965), vividly illustrates how complex, frustrating, and ultimately satisfying real-life negotiation can be. As an illustration, consider this happy ending to a world-shaking event:

In 1780 John Adams had been empowered by the Congress to negotiate peace with Great Britain and to become minister to the Court of St. James when peace was concluded. Five years later Adams arrived in London and for the first time met face-to-face with his bitter enemy of many years, George III. Adams, with great understatement, later wrote, "I felt more than I did or could express."

However, he delivered a formal address that included these sentiments: "the appointment of a public minister from the United States to Your Majesty's court will form an epoch in the history of England and of America." He was proud to be the first American citizen "to stand in Your Majesty's royal presence in a diplomatic character." He wished to be "instrumental in recommending my country . . . to Your Majesty's royal benevolence, and of restoring . . . the old good nature and good humor between people who . . . have the same language, a similar religion, and kindred blood." The King had the final and best word: "Sir, the circumstances of this audience are so extraordinary, the language you have discovered so justly adapted for the occasion, that I must say that I not only receive with pleasure the assurance of the friendly dispositions of the United States, but that I am very glad the choice has fallen upon you to be their minister . . . I will be very frank with you, I was the last to consent to the separation, but the separation having been made, and having become inevitable, I have always said, as I say now, that I would be the first to meet the friendship for the United States as an independent power."

Sail into the sunset, indeed! Instead, negotiate with your opposers as honorable human beings with differing needs and rejoice in your mutual victory.

Getting Down to Business

Although the Art of Negotiating® can be applied effectively to the personal, inter-organizational, and international levels, most of us are willing to leave the international level to the "experts" and tend to our immediate problems. Here are a few examples of how you might handle an opposer who confronts you with a win-or lose strategy.

> As a salesperson you want to employ a counterstrategy that will make the negotiation an "everybody wins" agreement.

Win-or-Lose Strategy 1

Your company is the sole supplier of a product to a major user. It is the only item you produce. Although it is essential that the buyer have the product, he uses his apparently strong negotiating position as a buyer to press constantly for price reductions, Feeling you have no recourse, you reluctantly give in, time and time again. Finally you reach the point where you break even.

Possible Counterstrategies

Use forbearance, a strategy of not responding immediately to the buyer's demands. Make time your ally. It makes little sense to rush toward another defeat. When you decide to confront the issue, slow production and wait for the purchaser's response. Like all counterstrategies, forbearance can backfire. Therefore, you need alternatives. You might try a reversal strategy. Announce that because your profit is so low, you plan to sell directly to the public via direct mail or to retailers, eliminating your customer from the market.

The countermoves can go on and on. If both sides are playing the win-or-lose game, the battle will only end when one side is exhausted and defeated. Time and money can be saved if both sides can be persuaded to work for a mutually satisfactory solution in which Everybody Wins®. A strong Everybody Wins® counterstrategy is to change levels, to rise from the level of personal involvement and switch to a statesmanlike overview. Work for a solution that will satisfy the needs of all parties. It is better to stop saying "I must have . . . ." and begin thinking and saying "We need . . . ."

Win-or-Lose Strategy 2

A major newspaper, in the process of negotiating a contract with the printers' union, is plagued with a new tactic. Instead of striking, the union begins to call "chapel meetings" that result in severe curtailment of production and loss of advertising revenues. As the meetings become more protracted, the newspaper is faced with a win-or-lose situation. It can give in to union demands or suffer increasing economic loss.

Possible Counterstrategies

The company can use the either/or strategy of setting limits—either the workers return to work full time or publication will be suspended by a certain date. With only two alternatives available, chances are both sides will emerge as losers.

A more constructive counterstrategy before holding a meeting might be for the union to use reversal—to offer to trade their right to hold "chapel meetings" for concessions from management, for example, methods for hearing and dealing with their grievances.

Win-or-Lose Strategy 3

In the salami strategy one side phases out its opposer while phasing itself in. One side takes a thin slice at a time until the whole salami has changed hands. The first slice seems too insignificant for anyone to make an issue of until it is too late. The salami strategy can be very frustrating to an inexperienced negotiator.

Possible Counterstrategies:

1. **Use forbearance.** Wait it out. Let your opposer slice away until you are ready to make your move. Then consider . . .

2. **Using reversal.** Let the opposer take so much that the scales tip over. Then . . .

3. **Use exposure.** Show that his motive is unbridled greed, not enlightened self-interest. You might also . . .

4. **Exact a penalty.** Make it clear that the price they will have to pay for the salami by the slice will get much higher per pound. The salami strategy, if properly used by an Everybody Wins® negotiator, can assist the negotiation process. For example, you can test your opposer's reactions. What limit will he place on the amount you may take? One slice? Two? Perhaps he will not resist your attempt to take the whole thing. It later proved that he didn't want any salami. He needed baloney.

You can also use the salami strategy to gain goodwill. If you are selling salami, don't pile too many slices on the scale at once and then remove some. Add to the pile until you reach the proper weight. You might even throw on an extra slice for good measure.

Win-or-Lose Strategy 4

The strategy of presenting nonnegotiable demands attempts to impose a stone wall between the negotiators. Each negotiator's motivation may be to show how strong he is, that his convictions are unalterable, or that his opposer should lower his expectations or reevaluate his demands. This strategy is difficult to counter head-on. It is probable that neither opposer will roll over and play dead, but each user of the strategy will regard any retreat on his part as an unacceptable loss of face.

Possible Counterstrategies:

1. **Hold behind-the-scene discussions.** The original demand is, after all, directed to the public as much as it is to the opposer.

2. **Get other people involved.** Mediators and arbitrators, both impartial outsiders, can effect changes that neither involved party could or would propose to or accept from the opposer.

3. **Use association.** Enlist the help of outsiders to bring pressure on the opposer. Nonnegotiable demands elicit strong pro or con reactions from the public. Rally those who support your stand.

4. **Practice forbearance.** Wait it out. No one can hold a defiant pose forever.

5. **While you are practicing forbearance, use your time profitably.** Try the salami strategy. While your opposer is busy protecting

> Pass over the demands and go on to other elements of the negotiation.

face, take some slices from the unguarded elements of the negotiation.

Win-or-Lose Strategy 5

As all strategies and tactics are, feinting is not in itself either morally "good" or morally "bad." The use it is put to will not necessarily decide the point either. In a win-or-lose game, the winner will call a tactic "good" and the loser, "bad." In an Everybody Wins® negotiation, however, both sides will call a strategy "good" if it helps them reach a consensus and "bad" if it impedes their progress. The test then becomes whether or not the feint helps produce a positive climate. A master salesperson uses feinting to gently nudge the negotiation back on course. Diplomats often do not have that freedom. Someone is always looking over their shoulders to make sure they stick to the straight and narrow path of "right" thinking. For example, on January 30, 1984, the U.S. chief negotiator for reducing strategic nuclear arms tried to sell the idea of getting the stalled arms-limitation talks going again. He suggested that the Soviet Union and the United States could "make a breakthrough" if the Russians would set a date for resuming the talks. A skilled negotiator might very well recognize the suggestion as feinting—diverting Russian attention from the stone wall they had erected to the benefits that might accrue if the wall were torn down. Not so the U.S. State Department.

The following day the Assistant Secretary of State for European Affairs attempted to set matters straight. He cautioned against expecting quick progress in the talks, saying, "We are prepared to begin negotiations right away. What the Soviets are willing to do is not clear." He warned of "the danger in the West of negotiating with ourselves," explaining that if the West were to show that it would steadily make concessions as long as the Soviet Union stayed away from the bargaining table, the Russians would have no incentive to return at all.

It was unclear exactly what the Assistant Secretary was trying to sell. At first glance it seemed to be the fear of everything: the chief negotiator, our allies, and, yes, even negotiation itself. Yet with whom were we to negotiate if not, first and foremost, our allies? A master negotiator of an earlier age had a better objective: "The only thing we have to fear is fear itself."

The only ones to escape attack were the Russians, who are, of course, "enigmatic." The only incentive offered to them was the possibility that if they did not return to the bargaining table every last missile would be installed in Europe. Yet this alone underlined the weakness of the U.S. negotiating stance.

The American negotiator had tried to use the threat of missile installation in Europe to get the arms-limitation talks moving. The feint did not work, the missiles went in, and the Russians walked out, as was their custom. The new attempt at a feint had actually become a *fait accompli*. Regardless of its name, a failed tactic should be discarded. It is a tool that is no longer useful to you. But before you can decide on a change, see how your new negotiating strategy can be workable in your own future.

> No creative negotiator would rely on a single tactic again and again.

Voices From the Past

A elderly man muttering to himself was once asked by his son: "Who are you talking to, Dad?" His reply: "To a sensible person for a change. One that doesn't ask damn foolish questions." Many salespeople, in their effort to get ahead, will accept advice for sales strategies from many different sources, amateur and professional.

Here are some of the people we turn to: professional experts, that is, lawyers, stockbrokers,

> Certainly, no one else knows our needs and aspirations better than we do.

psychiatrists, accountants, to whom we pay a fee, relatives such as father, mother, sister, brothers, uncles, and aunts, who gladly give advice away free, and friends and business associates, who probably expect payment in kind. One knowledgeable source of advice that we often ignore is ourself.

We all have our past experiences within us. When we negotiate with ourselves, it may be that we are actually looking for advice. How a negotiator integrates advice—his or her own and the outside world's—into his or her decisions needs examination.

Good advice should stimulate our remembrances of past experiences, even though the experiences may have occurred in an entirely different context or under a different set of circumstances. Both the giver and the receiver of advice must try to see that past experience can be an asset, but only if it is brought into accord with present realities. For example, giving a 10-year-old tomboy advice on how to deal with a love affair she may possibly have when she is 21 is not likely to be of much use to her. A few tips on making the Little League baseball team will be much more appreciated, especially if they work.

The value of the advice we receive cannot always be predicted accurately. Many professional advice givers, people who are paid to give advice, have no idea how to structure and present what they impart so that it is most meaningful to the receiver, and many receivers of professional advice do not know how to obtain the maximum benefit from their investment. Merely giving (or receiving) advice for 30 years does not necessarily give you 30 years of experience. It may be that you have repeated the same mistakes every year for those 30 years.

As human beings, it is impossible for us to experience everything. Much as we might like to promote only those experiences that reinforce the good aspects that we expect from life, it can't be done. Instead, we have numbers of choices. We want to make those choices so that we feel in control of our lives and satisfied that the judgments we make are meaningful, even if they are not infallible. Therefore, advice attempts to promote the choices that will fulfill our desires and needs in line with our basic philosophical desires.

Jumping the Barriers

Any experience can be meaningful for the balance of your life, the more so if you learn from it without making it an absolute barrier whose boundaries you never choose to test. Sometimes you may be so frightened or shocked by certain experiences that they become electrified fences within you. Although the time, circumstances, and level of involvement may change completely in later life, you may use this barrier to justify never again trying to expand your boundaries. This type of learning experience has a function but it must be understood and used wisely.

If something you did as a child resulted in your not becoming an artist, a singer, or a writer because your elementary school teacher, as an "expert," gave you a devastating mark, the experience should not limit you from trying again as an adult. Grandma Moses launched an amazing career as an artist at an age when most people have retired.

It would be presumptuous to attempt a definition of "true success," but an example of it appears in an inscription on a church near London:

> In the year 1653, when all things sacred in the kingdom
>
> Were either profaned or demolished,
>
> This church was build by Sir Richard Shirlye, Baronet,
>
> Whose singular praise it was
>
> To do the best things in the worst of thee.

Yet we must add a bit of cautionary advice: In 1653 the Church of England was no longer the state church. Englishmen, even Catholics, were given religious freedom. Jews, who had been driven out in 1290, were permitted to settle in England once more. Obviously, not everyone was unhappy. Perhaps Dickens' memorable opening lines in *A Tale of Two Cities* would be a more apt description of those days: "It was the best of times, it was the worst of times."

Nipping Problems in the Bud

In 1982 the Budd Company received a setback in its efforts to win a multimillion-dollar contract to build subway cars for New York City. The issues are too complex to go into here, but the setback came when U.S. Treasury Secretary Donald T. Regan agreed with the New York agency involved that Budd's rival, the Canadian firm, Bombardier, was "the superior bidder in terms of availability and cost of financing, the amount of work [to be] done in New York State, reliability of delivery and quality of design, engineering and performance . . . ."

There were other important charges (and there were countercharges), but the above list shows what a skilled negotiator would regard as a blueprint for a successful sales strategy. Budd apparently did not see it that way. Instead of attempting to work out a deal to satisfy the needs of both sides, it turned to the courts for relief.

Obviously, the apparent loss of a major contract by a U.S. company, albeit a subsidiary of a German firm, qualified as the "worst of times" for a number of American suppliers and workers. But how can we find "the best of times" in today's economic news? Certainly *not* by conducting "business as usual," *not* by satisfying our own needs at the expense of potential customers, and *not* by trying to get a larger piece of an ever-shrinking pie.

The Ever-expanding Pie

Now, more than ever, we need to perfect our negotiating skills and enhance our creative thinking skills. We need to make a bigger pie so that both sides will benefit and be satisfied. Cynics might (and do) say, "That's no pie. That's pie in the sky." Nonsense. Here is an example of having your pie (or cake) and eating it too.

An article by Dan Morgan and Walter Pincus (The *Washington Post*, July 6, 1982) describes how Northrop Corp. did it. Northrop, the fighter plane manufacturer, was confronted with the same problems that beset businesses around the world: aggressive (and hungry) competitors, buyers deep in debt and short of funds, and scaled-down U.S. aid and credits.

Northrop decided that the way to overcome these obstacles was to work with potential customers to expand their revenues so they could afford to buy planes. One way seemed promising—expand the country's exports with the help of Northrop's worldwide network of representatives. It worked.

In the early 1970s, Northrop initiated its program of "offsets" in a deal with the Swiss government. It wanted to sell $450 million of F5E planes to Switzerland. In exchange, Northrop promised to find markets for $136 million worth of Swiss products. To quote from the article:

"It [Northrop] set up a special office in Switzerland, inventoried 800 Swiss companies and established a computerized library of exportable Swiss products at Northrop headquarters in California. Finally, Northrop representatives all over the world were told to be alert to markets for the Swiss products . . . Within five years Northrop helped 200 Swiss companies find markets for $209 million worth of their products, mostly in countries other than the United States."

This last fact is important. As a Northrop spokesman explained: "We're creating jobs here in the U.S. We feel we cut into the U.S. market at a minimum because we focus on exports to third countries." When the article was written, Northrop had sold planes and $30 million worth of Canadian paper cups to Nigeria, Swiss elevators to Egypt, and Swiss precision drills to Spain, among other items, and was working on a deal to sell Turkish wines, refrigerators, and other products.

Bigger pies, anyone?

> Try to look for alternatives. Instead of the "best" or the "worst," you might find something that's pretty good.

You can obtain as much advice as your purse and your patience will tolerate. But you must be willing to take a broad view of your problems and consider the many possible solutions that are open to you before deciding upon an answer. In that way you have a much better chance of acting wisely. If you don't—well, think of La Rochefoucauld's observation: "Old people like to give good advice as solace for no longer being able to provide bad examples."

Key Points

A man who wants to hang you one day may, through the magic of negotiation, become a good friend the next. No tactic is indispensable, but be sure you have a stronger alternative available before you discard the old tactic. Advice should not only be good but it should be good for something. Life fulfillment and shortcuts are mutually contradictory terms. In a tight situation you should not concentrate on Why? but on Whom? and What?

Win-or-lose negotiators will insist they want performance rather than statements of intention until they see the hangman's noose. In a successful negotiation, things of value are exchanged, not appropriated by one side.

Disclosure: Sales Clincher or Cliché

9

Disclosure: Sales Clincher or Cliché

"Talking about oneself can also be the means to conceal oneself."

Nietzsche, Beyond Good and Evil, 1886

Disclosure is an essential part of any sales negotiation. Wittingly or unwittingly, disclosure will create a negotiating climate, establish the direction of the negotiation, determine price, and bring about a conclusion, along with many other services and/or disservices. In the hands of an amateur it can ensure failure. An amateur salesperson uses clichés as all-purpose substitutes for genuine disclosure. "You know what I mean" gives his opposer carte blanche to decide what the "facts" are. "I'll tell you what I'm gonna do" does not signal that the bluebird of happiness is nigh. "That's my final offer" can just as easily signal the start of a negotiation as the abrupt termination of one.

To many people, even the suggestion that they disclose valuable information sounds, at best, idealistic and at worst, downright subversive. Instead of the expansive "open covenants . . . openly arrived at," they ask, "Does Macy's tell Gimbels?" This is understandable in a society where behavior in many areas is equated with purely adversary relationships. In such a climate any disclosure is (and probably should be) regarded as placing a loaded gun in the hand of your enemy.

Why Disclose Anything?

Possibly the best argument in favor of disclosure, and certainly the briefest, is Benjamin Disraeli's remark, "Ignorance never settles a question." To be most effective, the disclosure must be made only after your competence as a negotiator has been established. Then a

> A master salesperson regards disclosure as an important tool that can dispel ignorance and settle the question.

negotiation can be moved off dead center. If a disclosure is timely and made in a straightforward, believable, trusting manner, it can produce movement, perhaps toward reciprocal disclosure and ultimately to a climate of trust that will produce an agreement that settles the question.

On the other hand, if you intentionally attempt to leave your opposers in ignorance of what you perceive as the "true" situation, you are less likely to achieve your objective. At best, your opposer will be bewildered. At worst, she may feel conned and ready for revenge. In any event, the "agreement" will be distorted, If there is a winner, it could be a third party.

Indeed, the failure to disclose can benefit third parties without their even knowing what the "truth" is. In her 1933 biography of British Empire Builder Cecil Rhodes, Sarah Gertrude Millin notes: "There are more Rhodes Scholars from America than from all the British Dominions put together." That is probably still true today, although this was hardly Rhodes' intent when he provided two scholarships for each state. None of his flunkies had dared tell him the truth that at the time of his death in 1902 there were 45 states in the Union. Rhodes firmly believed that the United States still consisted of the 13 original colonies.

When To Disclose

When to disclose is important, but many people devote more time to that consideration than they do to finding the facts they want to disclose. This is usually due to self-dramatization. Suddenly they are sure they, and only they, possess the "truth". Therefore, facts are unimportant. With nothing but the "truth" to communicate, they are unable to reach out and help others to reach a satisfactory consensus. This is one quality of win-or-lose negotiators. They know what they want, and they couldn't care less about the other side's needs.

Consider the gas station attendant who said to a reporter during a gasoline shortage when odd or even license plates were serviced only on correspondingly odd or even days, "If he's that stupid, and he waits in line an hour and doesn't know the rules, I let him get to the pump, and then I break his heart." It is difficult to see how even the attendant benefited from this negotiation. He didn't even get a sale.

The timing of a disclosure should be determined by when the facts presented will provide maximum benefits, not to a single individual but to the group as a whole. Each set of circumstances will dictate its own proper timing, and your recognition of the proper time to disclose will be determined by how well you have prepared for the negotiation.

For example, the 1974 wage negotiation for the U.S. steel industry was preceded by an "experimental negotiating agreement," a negotiation that prepared the way for the wage negotiations. The agreement barred strikes or lockouts, guaranteed a wage increase of at least 3 percent, and provided for binding arbitration. It sounds so sensible and civilized that the novice might think it had sprung full-blown from the mind of an experienced negotiator. The concept may have, but not the acceptance of it. Acceptance depended on the proper timing of a set of disclosures.

By the union:

1. It would not strike.

2. It would accept a relatively low floor for wages, from which it would then negotiate.

3. It would agree to binding arbitration.

By management:

1. There would be no lockout.

2. There would be a wage increase of at least 3 percent.

3. It would agree to arbitration.

At the beginning of any sales negotiation there is almost always a great gap dividing the two sides. Competent sales negotiators slowly and carefully try to narrow the gap by giving and receiving concessions. The resulting agreement may never seem completely satisfactory to either side. What both see is a slow but steady reduction of their share of the pie.

> The master salesperson tries to minimize the "sacrifices" and maximize the benefits, not by using "accepted business practices" to reach a compromise but by realizing when it is time for creative selling and buying.

Where To Disclose

Where to disclose is closely linked with when to disclose. Indeed, the master salesperson, recognizing that time and place are one, will not concede that there is a difference. Most amateurs and even some competent salespeople overemphasize the importance of "where," making the site more important than the content of the disclosure.

A perfect match of "where" and "when" can, however, produce a solution to seemingly insurmountable problems. Abigail Adams Homans, a descendant of two U.S. Presidents, once combined "where" and "when" to produce a victory for herself and no real damage to her opposer. A resident of Boston, she was caught one night in a severe snowstorm, so she went to the awesome Somerset Club, of which her husband was a member, and demanded a room. The desk clerk refused, citing a club rule that an unaccompanied woman could not occupy a room. "In that case," said Mrs.

Homans, "I'll go out and get my cab driver." She got a room and spent a quiet, unaccompanied night.

In those allegedly strong negotiating situations where someone makes "an offer you can't refuse," consider the example of a Washington, D.C., bus driver: where not to disclose. One night the driver had three unruly customers in the back of the bus. In time they came to the front and announced they were taking over the bus. The driver set the hand brake·and got off. The three men could not figure out how to release the brake so they returned to the rear of the bus and sat down. The driver got back on, released the brake, and continued on his route. Ten blocks later the three again came to the front and announced they were taking over. The driver set the hand brake and got out. The men then began pressing buttons at random in hopes of releasing the brake. They did not succeed, but one button closed the door and another set off flashing lights that signaled the police the driver was in trouble. When the police came, the men could not even locate the button to open the door. Moral: Whether your scene is a bus or a business, make sure you are an experienced director before you try to take over, and that you know what is called for.

How To Disclose

A disclosure might be defined as presenting "facts" hitherto unknown to the listener. A master salesperson will add a footnote: Disclosure can strengthen a relationship and enhance the possibility of reaching a lasting, mutually beneficial agreement. There are, of course, other types of disclosure. One is the ego-satisfying citation of "facts" by a know-it-all. This kind of disclosure is likely to inspire the reaction elicited from Samuel Johnson in another context: "It [a dog's ability to walk on two legs] is not done well, but you are surprised to find it done at all."

Two other types, *exposés* and *revelations*, may have a ripple effect on the outside world, but they are usually not intended to change relationships for the better on a one-to-one basis.

Exposés tend to be self-serving and are more likely to wreck relationships than improve them. For example, a young woman in trouble with the law in Memphis, Tennessee, called a news conference to reveal she had had sexual encounters with an astonishing number of Memphis policemen. The police department was certainly not benefited by the exposé. The public may have been titillated and the woman, judging from her meta-talk (hidden meaning), may have gained a temporary advantage. She excused her conduct by saying she "just liked and respected officers of the law." The use of "just" is reminiscent of the song that begins, "I'm just a little girl from Little Rock. . . ." It attempts to minimize her own culpability and implies that the officers abused her trust.

Revelations, once "received from on high," are used to stir masses of people, sometimes for good ends, sometimes for bad, depending upon your point of view. They are the epitome of the "win-or-lose" negotiating philosophy, as exemplified by a long history of religious wars, "righteous" causes, and more recently, advertising fervor.

Disclosures are not made only by verbal admissions. They can be unintentional. The master salesperson is quick to seize on gestures and meta-talk that convey emotional reactions that the opposer might hesitate to put into words. This can establish a rapport that eliminates the need to verbalize a number of disclosures and makes the important ones easier to articulate.

Key Points

Disclosure is so important to the negotiation process that its many aspects have been considered:

- Why disclose
- Where to disclose
- How to disclose
- When to disclose

Disclosure is not yet finished. The next chapter will complete the process with What to Disclose.

What To Disclose

What To Disclose

10

"The greatest cunning is to have none at all."

Carl Sandburg, The People, Yes, 1936

The subject matter of disclosures can be as varied as the objectives of negotiations. Disclosures can, however, be grouped in at least three categories: preconditional, goodwill offering, and tit for tat.

Preconditional Disclosures

Disclosures demanded by one side as a precondition to negotiation are common in every type of relationship. "Tell me how much you love me and I'll give you a kiss." "Before I buy I want to know how much the business is *really* worth." "Wash your hands or you don't get any dinner." "If you have to ask the price, you can't afford it." All of these have a whiff of blackmail about them and are not conducive to fruitful negotiation. Reconditional disclosures, however, do play a role, not necessarily in the actual negotiation but in preparation for it. The agenda is, after all, a set of stated or implied preconditions. In the preliminary stage of negotiation they can clear the air, remove ambiguities, and reveal items that require expert negotiating efforts.

Goodwill Disclosures

People, especially amateur negotiators, disclose information as a gesture of good will. Without establishing the proper foundation, all too often these efforts are unfocused and do not produce the desired feeling of trust in the opposer. Anita Counihan (better known as the actress and fashion model Anita Colby) made this mistake when young. "I remember saying to some man, 'Hi, my name is Anita Counihan, and I'm 19 and I'm a model. And what do you do?' So he said, 'I'm Vincent Astor, and that's my yacht out there.' Boy, was I innocent."

Even the experienced negotiator can be trapped into disclosing irrelevant, misleading, or even false information. For example, British Prime Minister Edward Heath felt he could risk his government by calling for new elections in 1974 and disclosing the "truth." Plagued by a coal miners' strike that resisted all his negotiating efforts, he went to the voters with the news that the miners were already earning 3 percent more than workers in manufacturing and, therefore, their new wage demands were excessive. The voters "bought" his argument and Heath seemed headed for a decisive victory.

However, only days before the election, the National Pay Board disclosed that Heath's figures were in error. The miners actually earned 8 percent less, not 3 percent more. The whole

> Be sure of the facts you disclose, otherwise they will dispose of you.

rationale for the election—government against extremist union leaders—was wiped out. Also wiped out was the Conservative majority in the House of Commons.

Tit-For-Tat Disclosures

In sales negotiating, both the preconditional and the goodwill offering categories of disclosure have limited value. The master salesperson knows that a more precise tool is required. The tit-for-tat type of disclosure can be such a tool. To be completely effective, however, the other aspects of the negotiating process must be integrated into a perfectly orchestrated whole. Then both sides can be confident of each other's ability and an uninhibited exchange of information can take place.

For a successful interaction of two master salespeople two things are required:

1. feelings must exist such that there need be no contradictory body language or meta-talk

2. the climate must be such that it inspires a cooperative effort to reach a successful conclusion

A master salesperson is also aware that information disclosed need not be earthshaking, but it must be significant to be effective and to achieve the desired resolution of a problem. Even an ordinary life situation can be resolved more easily if the most advanced negotiating techniques are used.

A few years ago John Corry, writing in the *New York Times*, offered a good example. An owner of a printing house in lower Manhattan had hired a male secretary who not only had a pleasant personality but also was a very capable worker. Since good secretaries are hard to come by, the owner asked the young man if there was anything that would make his job more pleasant. After some thought, the secretary admitted that he would like to wear dresses to work. Adding up the pluses and minuses, the owner said it was fine with him. For a time the other workers made rude remarks, but after the novelty wore off, they accepted the situation. The secretary was happy in his work, and the owner had a loyal and competent secretary.

Several elements of this successful negotiation might be noted. First, the owner disclosed that he was very happy with the secretary's work and wanted to keep him, thus creating a supportive climate. This encouraged the employee to make a reciprocal disclosure, based upon a feeling of trust, a disclosure that few employers would have accepted with equanimity. By calmly considering the proposition, thus creating a relaxed climate, the owner disclosed that he still trusted and accepted the employee. Thus the negotiation could end happily for both sides.

As the master salesperson often finds, there can be fringe benefits in the successful solution to a problem. In this case the owner later remarked, "Actually, he doesn't look bad at all."

As a rule, two master negotiators should be able to reach a settlement very quickly, going directly to the heart of the problem and wasting no time on extraneous matters. Each side will promptly realize that the opposer is a master, and that a quick solution will be forthcoming.

If you observe master negotiators closely, you'll soon discover that they do not play a negotiating "game." Rather, they practice the Art of Negotiation®. They know that it is necessary to find a common ground and avoid the pitfalls of a competitive "I must win the game" attitude. At the earliest possible moment in negotiations, each side will disclose the maximum concessions it is willing to make and the minimum concessions that are expected in return This is not always explicit. Such disclosures are often done subtly, by innuendo, and sometimes by deliberate tipoffs. These skills and techniques, arrived at through long experience and training, enable master negotiators to reach satisfactory settlements quickly.

Examples of this type of negotiation occur daily at the United Nations. However, remember that the final decisions are not within the control of those professionals. Diplomats act as agents for their governments. They are not permitted to effect satisfactory settlements of world problems by themselves.

The final distinction is that master negotiators not only possess all the necessary knowledge and experience, but also maintain a personal philosophy based on ethical concerns, a philosophy that enables them to conclude negotiations in a manner completely satisfactory to parties on all sides of the issues. Negotiation is a useful tool of human behavior. The Art of Negotiation® can be mastered with study and practice.

To show you how far short of the ideal we have fallen in the past, here is a quotation from *How Nations Negotiate*, by Fred Charles Ikle:

> The compleat [sic] negotiator, according to seventeenth and eighteenth-century manuals on diplomacy, should have a quick mind but unlimited patience, know how to dissemble without being a liar, inspire trust without trusting others, be modest but assertive, charm others without succumbing to their charm, and possess plenty of money and a beautiful wife while remaining indifferent to all temptation of riches and women.

No wonder master negotiators are such a rare commodity!

Key Points

This chapter ends the material on disclosure. What to disclose has been divided into three categories:

1. Preconditional

2. Good Will

3. Tit-for-Tat

Think of the many opportunities you had for these types of disclosures. Try not to miss any in your future negotiating.

Climates: Worst-Case and Best-Case Studies

Climates: Worst-Case and Best-Case Studies

"Adapt yourself to the environment in which your lot has been cast, and show true love to the fellow mortals with whom destiny has surrounded you."

Marcus Aurelius, Meditations (2nd century A.D.)

"If way to the Better there be, it exacts a full look at the Worst."

Thomas Hardy

When participants in my Art of Negotiating® seminars are asked whether they prefer to be "sold" or self-motivated in reaching a decision, self-motivation wins hands down. In a way, this is astonishing. Here are top executives from around the world, most of them master salespeople, who seem to be rejecting a vital tool of their trade.

There is more shadow than substance to this point of view. "Selling," in itself, is not a dirty word. Used in the context of a negative climate, however, it can indeed be defined as trying to gain control of another's point of view by persuading, convincing, or influencing. The salesperson is viewed as determined to be a "winner" and never mind if the buyer is a "loser." Your reactions as a buyer, in turn, are predictable: "I become defensive," "I fight harder," "I get aggressive," "I become more determined," "I dig my heels in."

Only rarely someone says, "I don't get too upset. That's the way it should be done."

When asked how you would react to a salesperson who states that he would like to work with you on a problem without preconceptions and with the aim of reaching a mutually satisfactory agreement, a typical reaction might be "What's he trying to sell me this time?" In other words, the first approach makes a person defensive—the second, suspicious. Neither climate is likely to result in profit or satisfaction for either side.

When we, as salespeople, encounter these reactions in real life, we shouldn't attribute them to innate perversity but rather to our own inadequacy and lack of negotiating skills. Most of us are pragmatists, and we usually are in a hurry. We use any shortcut we can to achieve the results we want. In many life situations this is sensible. For example, we feel no obligation to give detailed instructions to a short-order cook when we want a hamburger with french fries. (If we do, we may live to regret it.)

Sales negotiation should be an art for life fulfillment, not a skill for getting your way, with extra points for speed. Otherwise, your opposers may feel they are in the position of the man who wanted to buy an exotic bird:

The pet-shop proprietor brought out a huge bird with formidable talons and a beak capable of cracking a coconut shell with one blow.

"But can he talk?" asked the customer.

"Of course. Say something to the gentleman, Polly."

"Polly wants a cracker and *damned* quick."

The frankness of Polly's disclosure plus Polly's appearance left no doubt as to the bird's sincerity. Yet a sound long-term relationship seems improbable.

No rational person would ever claim that sales negotiations are easy, although a surprising number believe that there is such a thing as a "born salesperson." There are, indeed, such people. By birth and/or brains and talent they fit into a circumscribed group of wealthy, powerful people who can advance their own interests as well as those of others. For a born salesperson, winning comes with the territory. Losers, of course, are excluded from or cast out of the magic circle. When this happens, "everyone" knows exactly how it happened. Willy Loman, remember, got a couple of spots on his hat and was finished.

So much for mythology. Let's see what "really" happened. It is axiomatic that when you play hard ball you're going to win some and lose some. You can blame your loss on whatever you like—your

> Only when you view negotiation as a process can you acknowledge that your ultimate success or failure was inevitable.

choice of reasons is endless and each may have been a factor. Will that realization help you? Of course not. Isolated facts will neither cure nor comfort you.

Samuel Johnson once said, "Depend upon it, sir, when a man knows he is to be hanged in a fortnight, it concentrates his mind wonderfully." He was right. So, instead of an "ordinary" sales negotiation, let's concentrate on two negotiations where the time, place, and manner of death or freedom were on the table. Both involved the fate of hostages and, as it turned out, many others, including a U.S. president, were profoundly affected. In one case, no one "won." In the other, everybody did.

Worst Case: American Hostages in Iran

For a master negotiator, perhaps the most challenging fact about a hostage situation is that everything seems stripped down to bare essentials. Unlike less bizarre negotiations, there is usually no long-term preparation. One is suddenly confronted with a *fait accompli* and surrounded by an uncertain, alien climate. Tactics and strategies that have "always" worked for the immediate participants appear to achieve little or nothing.

When American hostages seized in Iran during the Carter administration were finally released, they told of their behavior during captivity, of their random acts of defiance and surreptitious ways of gaining information that seemed so important to them then but had no value once they were freed. The hostages themselves were, in truth, "naked to [their] enemies," because a hostage is only rarely a competent negotiator.

In the initial period of hostage taking, differing negotiating techniques and philosophies begin to emerge. The Iranian situation, due in part to its complexity and duration, offered fascinating examples of the three levels of negotiating expertise. For the moment, let us set aside considerations of what is necessary for the master negotiator to succeed and examine some of the negotiating techniques and philosophies that emerged.

> It is easy for the trained observer to separate the amateurs from the competent negotiators. If the hostages are very lucky, a master negotiator may emerge to take over the process.

A long, confidential cable sent to the U.S. Secretary of State by the *charge d'affaires* at the U.S. Embassy in Teheran several months before the seizure of the hostages will help us gain an insight into U.S. views on negotiating with the Iranians. Here are quoted excerpts, with emphasis added and with comments in brackets from The Art of Negotiating® point of view:

Subject: Negotiations

"We believe the underlying cultural and psychological qualities that account for the nature of these difficulties are and will remain relatively constant." [This is an attempt by a nontrained psychologist in an inadequate time frame to figure out the *Why* of the opposer's psychological negotiating reasons. The master negotiator would report *Who* is doing *What*.]

"Perhaps the single dominant aspect of the Iranian psyche is an overriding egoism. Its antecedents lie in the long Iranian history of instability and insecurity which put a premium on self-preservation. The practical effect of it is an almost total Iranian preoccupation with self and leaves little room for understanding points of view other than one's own." [Again, an amateur psychological approach.]

"The reverse of this particular psychological coin, and having the same historical roots as Iranian egoism, is a pervasive unease about the nature of the world in which one lives. The Iranian experience has been that nothing is permanent and it is commonly perceived that hostile forces abound. In such an environment each individual must be constantly alert for opportunities to protect himself or herself against the malevolent forces that would otherwise be his or her undoing. He or she is obviously justified in using almost any means available to exploit such opportunities. This approach underlies the so-called bazaar mentality so common among Iranians, a mind-set that often ignores longer term interests in favor of immediately obtainable advantages and countenances practices that are regarded as unethical by other norms." [This entire paragraph deals with straw men: (a) nothing is permanent, (b) hostile forces abound, (c) bazaar mentality, (d) countenances practices that are regarded as unethical by other norms. These are offered as premises, as though they are exclusively Iranian and that we in the United States start from better assumptions.]

"The Iranian proclivity for assuming that to say something is to do it. . . ." [No one in the United States would be short of examples of telling, or even ordering, people to do things without being obeyed.]

". . . [T]here are the Iranian concepts of influence and obligation . . . only grudgingly bestowed and then just to the extent that a tangible *quid pro quo* is immediately perceptible." [Many American negotiators would consider this in line with their concept of compromise.]

These inadequate premises are followed by six "principles" of negotiation. There are several lessons for those who would negotiate with Iranians in all this:

First, one should never assume that his or her side of the issue will be recognized, let alone that it will be conceded to have merits. Iranian preoccupation with self precludes this. A negotiator must force recognition of his or her position upon his or her Iranian opposite number.

Second, one should not expect an Iranian to readily perceive the advantages of a long-term relationship based upon trust. He or she will assume that his or her opposite number is essentially an adversary. In dealing with him or her, he or she will attempt to maximize the benefits to himself or herself that are immediately obtainable. He or she will be prepared to go to great lengths to achieve this goal, including running the risk of so alienating whomever he or she is dealing with that future business would be unthinkable, at least to the latter.

Third, interlocking relationships of all aspects of an issue must be painstakingly, forcefully, and repeatedly developed. Linkages will be neither readily comprehended nor accepted by Iranian negotiators.

Fourth, one should insist on performance as the *sine qua non* at each stage of negotiations.

Fifth, cultivation of good will for good will's sake is a waste of effort. The overriding objective at all times

> Statements of intention count for almost nothing.

should be impressing upon the Iranian across the table the mutuality of the proposed undertakings. He or she must be made to know that a *quid pro quo* is involved on both sides.

Finally, one should be prepared for the threat of breakdown in negotiations at any given moment and not be surprised by the possibility. Given the Iranian negotiator's cultural and psychological limitations, he or she is going to resist the very concept of a rational (from the Western point of view) negotiating process.

If the other side in a negotiation used these six principles in negotiating with you, how long would you tolerate it?

Afterthought: Afterthought makes clear that these types of guidelines to *any* negotiation are almost surely doomed to failure. At the time the confidential cable was written, there was constant agitation by Marxist guerrillas outside the U.S. Embassy. Ironically, forces loyal to the Ayatollah Khomeini had rescued the Embassy staff from an attempted seizure in February 1980.

As a result, there seemed ample time before the hostages were actually taken to philosophize about the strange ways of Iranians—"overriding egotism," "an almost total preoccupation with self" and a "pervasive unease about the nature of the world"—as though America and Americans were devoid of these traits. Instead of making blanket statements about the Iranians, American observers would have served our negotiations better if they had provided detailed observations of the revolution that was in process— the people, forces, and results. This would have provided a sound foundation for the negotiations that inevitably followed.

Instead of the thorough preparation for successful and beneficial negotiation that a master negotiator would have insisted on, the man in charge of the embassy was content with preparations for a game of "Them Against Us."

Stalemate and Sideshows: President Carter's first overall strategy, forbearance, was continued with few exceptions throughout the long crisis. From its beginning, Carter made efforts to set up meetings between his Secretary of State and Iran's Foreign Minister, enlisting the help of United Nations officials as agents with limited authority. Just when Carter's effort seemed about to succeed, Ayatollah Khomeini refused to let his Foreign Minister leave the country. There followed a stream of self-appointed envoys, amateurs who attempted (unsuccessfully) to prove that anyone can negotiate a deal.

Carter also adopted the establishment of limits as a tactic to force Iran to move. Iran's assets were frozen and its oil was barred from the United States. The International Court of Justice and the U.N. Security Council were asked to demand the release of the hostages. A U.N. commission was set up to go to Iran, but its efforts at negotiating failed when the Ayatollah decreed that the Iranian Parliament would decide the hostages' fate. This was not to happen for many months.

As efforts to counter forbearance by the other side, Carter temporarily made his forbearance strategy more costly: He severed diplomatic relations, shut off most trade with Iran, and pressed his European allies to join the boycott. He also approved a risky and badly planned military rescue operation, accepting the probability that 15 hostages would die in the effort. The effort failed, and eight U.S. servicemen were lost. With resigned fatalism, the Carter administration settled down to wait for the election of a new Iranian Parliament.

Why the forbearance stalemate? A review of the essential preliminary steps in negotiation provides at least some of the answers.

1. **Get to know your opposer.** We have seen the stereotypes that dominated the thinking of at least one diplomat. Coupled with this was an almost complete ignorance in the United States of what the opponents of the Shah were doing. The United States accepted the Shah's estimate of his own worth and invulnerability and ignored the forces that were to overthrow him.

2. **Discovering the needs of the opposer.** After years of almost obsequious attention to every wish of the Shah, American diplomats, when confronted with the

conflicting groups trying to control Iran, could only paraphrase Freud: "The great question which I have not been able to answer, despite my years of research into the Iranian soul, is, What do the Iranians want?"

This should have been the first question asked. This never came to pass. Ayatollah

> Discovery of your opposer's needs is basic to any negotiation.

Khomeini was also badly informed. The end, which was no end, was a loss for all. Each side neither got to know the other, nor had the opportunity to use the full negotiation process.

A conclusion that would have established a needed ongoing relationship between the parties would have been a success for all.*

Best Case: The Hostage in a Bogotá Embassy

In sharp contrast to the everybody-loses negotiation in Iran, the seizure of the Dominican Republic Embassy in Colombia and the subsequent negotiation that resulted in the freeing of the hostages was a dazzling success. The needs of both sides were understood and, for the most part, met. There were no losers, only winners. Late in February 1980, 16 Colombian guerrillas, 10 men and 6 women, seized the Dominican Republic's Embassy in Bogotá during a reception. More than 20 hostages, including 14 ambassadors, were held hostage. The guerrillas demanded the release of 311 comrades from Colombian jails. (Most of the hostages were held for 61 days. The Uruguayan ambassador escaped, causing a colleague to say, "He was a traitor to the pact we made to stick together. Afterward, they doubled internal security and took away some of the liberties we did have.")

Kathy Sawyer in The *Washington Post* summarized what happened inside the Embassy:

*Now, after the Gulf War, we find that we could have learned much from our dealings with Iran that might have served us well in promoting our understanding of Iraq.

Diego Asencio, who was the U.S. ambassador, and the ambassadors of Mexico and Brazil joined forces to develop a rapport with their young, publicity-conscious captors during the 61-day standoff and, offering their services as expert consultants, managed to help write the terms of their own release. While they were determinedly active mentally and physically, they reported that other hostages became passive, vegetated and withered.

Asencio said that he believes his ability to communicate with his captors on various levels was crucial in saving his life. Even his circumstances of birth provided a tactical weapon against his captors in their lengthy political debates. As the son of a Spanish-born laborer, he told them, "You are the bourgeoisie and I am the worker's son."

Smart, Not Tough: Other quotes of the U.S. diplomat give insights into the mind of a master sales negotiator.

It was a fascinating experience. I cherish it in many ways. I wouldn't want to repeat it, but, you know, how often do you have an opportunity to live with guys like that for 61 days and see them function?

Asked how he would have felt about a military attempt to rescue him:

I felt it would result in considerable casualties. With my colleagues, I decided instead of getting tough, let's get smart. We have the experience. They have the muscles, the grenades, the dynamite, the bombs.

Of his relationship with the guerrillas:

I thought it important to make friends with them and make it more difficult for them to kill us. But also, perhaps, to create some doubts in their minds about their ideological approach.

From time to time, the guerrillas would go out and negotiate and then come back and tell us and ask us for our advice. And it was often taken.

At one point, they planned a harsh diatribe to introduce their demands. We convinced them it was completely unacceptable and would foul up the negotiations and that they would be taken for savages. Whereupon they asked us for a first draft of what we would say and we provided it. And that was the beginning of the successful negotiations.

We convinced them that the exchange of political prisoners they were asking for would put them in the category of mere bank robbers. We persuaded them they could help create a historic agreement, something that would be helpful and would give them a rather statesmanlike cast. That was a rather tough one to sell, but they finally accepted it.

A Goodbye Kiss

The *New York Times* summarized the final results:

Challenged to defend both its international ties and its domestic legitimacy the Government emerged with both enhanced. It was firm on principles but restrained and flexible in its tactics, thus protecting the hostages without surrendering to extortion. When the guerrillas demanded the release of imprisoned comrades, the Government accelerated some legal procedures but refused any wholesale release of potentially dangerous terrorists. It denied the guerrillas any official payment of ransom, but, having made the point, consented to a privately arranged payment. And in a step that may have decided the issue, it agreed to let the Inter-American Human Rights Commission monitor prison conditions and the trials of terrorists.

There were tears and embraces when the diplomats and their captors parted, and Asencio kissed one of the female guerillas goodbye—as good a way as any to end a negotiation. In both hostage situations everyone was negotiating constantly. In one case they did it well. Some final observations may be in order.

In both situations American diplomats attempted to "sell" something, and in a sense, both succeeded. In Iran, the diplomat "sold" his superiors in Washington a bill of goods, in the meantime ignoring the real needs of his opposers in the impending negotiation.

The resulting climate of suspicion, distrust, and American "superiority" has endured to this day. In Bogotá, the American created a climate of cooperation and trust that permitted an exchange of things of value beneficial to both sides.

Key Points

In considering climates from the view of worst case and best case, try to put yourself into these negotiating situations. How would you have behaved?

Prisoner or Free Agent? The Choice is Yours

12

Prisoner or Free Agent? The Choice is Yours

"Everything that is really great and inspiring is created by the individual who can labor in freedom."

Albert Einstein, Out of My Later Years, 1950

"How can we personalize our wedding? With the possible exception of the Princess of Wales, who mistook her bridegroom's name during the wedding ceremony, those involved in weddings usually have enough sense of the identity of the participants to make distinguishing gimmicks unnecessary."

Miss Manners, The *Washington Post*, May 6, 1984

In fairness to the newlyweds, Miss Manners might have added a caveat: In any negotiation, an introduction is only the starting move. The hard work lies ahead.

It in no way minimizes the importance of the salesperson to observe that most sales negotiations lend themselves to solutions where everyone wins. One reason is that they most frequently take place on the inter-organizational level. This tends to create a dispassionate climate in which each party is basically free to change or adhere to an initial position unimpeded by personal needs. (Compare this with Willy Loman's overwhelming personal need for "respect" in an indifferent world.) In spite of this perceived advantage, however, many buyers and/or sellers believe it is not good enough. They want more.

Winner Takes All

A few years ago an Indiana farmer made headlines: he was broke and $35 million in debt. A possible clue to his initial success and ultimate failure was his boast when the sheriff handed him a document: "This is the first summons I haven't been able to negotiate my way out of."

Unfortunately for American business, the farmer is not the only high roller to so circumscribe the role of negotiator. Many top buyers and sellers, in their search for quick, short-term success, have managed to "win" for themselves at the expense of their companies, their associates, and society in general. The farmer summed up the driving force behind his actions: "When you never lose, it's hard to quit. It's like heads you win, tails you win. That's the way I like to play."

Unfortunately, so do many others in the business world. In all fairness it should be noted that some salespeople have also become addicted to zero-sum games. The success of David Mamet's play, *Glengarry Glen Ross*, attests to that. This should come as no surprise. The traveling salesman stories of a more innocent age have been elevated to the status of accepted wisdom in many of our institutes of higher learning. In *Life and Death on the Corporate Battlefield* (New York: Simon and Schuster, 1982), Paul Solman and Thomas Friedman examine the way the Harvard Graduate School of Business Administration teaches students how to "develop a killer instinct." They explain: "Competitive game playing and winning is a very serious business here." One course deals with variations of the classic Prisoner's Dilemma game.

> There are probably many salespersons alive today who will tell you horror stories of what it's like to deal with buyers who insist on winning everything.

These are the rules of one game offered in the course:

1. There are two players.

2. They play only once.

3. They each have two choices: cooperate or defect.

4. They do not know the other's choice until the game is over.

5. If both decide to cooperate they each win $5.

6. If one cooperates and the other defects, the cooperator loses $5 and the defector wins $10.

7. If they both defect they both lose $2.

The dilemma, of course, is that if both defect, both will do much worse than if they'd had cooperated. What the "winner" needs is a sucker, because those who believe in "survival of the fittest" also believe you should never give a sucker an even break. Since the game is played only once, every "rational" player will defect and no one will win.

Even if the game is played, say, 20 times, "logic" would demand that both sides defect on every move. The reason? Both sides suddenly find themselves playing a game of chicken over and over. Each player "knows" that on the twentieth move, the other is going to defect so each "has to" defect on the nineteenth move to "win." Then in lockstep both march back to the first move, where both defect. (It should be noted that if both sides defect on every move, each will lose $40 in an attempt to win $10.) Even the course instructor conceded that this was carrying logic to an extreme.

The Dilemma of Negotiating

One definition of "dilemma" is a choice between equally unsatisfactory alternatives. Very few business entrepreneurs would passively accept the logical (and they *are* logical) alternatives presented by the Prisoner's Dilemma. Creative alternatives that offer better (winning) choices must, and will, be found. As we have seen, Harvard MBA's were taught to develop "a killer instinct."

Salespeople, except for those in bucket shops or similar operations, often have difficulty reconciling their self-image with zero-sum game playing. For them, the concept that the only good buyer is a dead one is not only illogical— but insane. However, they are afraid of being called wimps if they say so. They are possibly wrong in their

> However much moralists may deplore it, many business executives have prospered mightily by "knocking off" their opposers. Lethal weapons are not necessary. Negotiating to win a zero-sum game will often do quite well.

first assumption and probably right in the second. What the MBA student and the irresolute salesperson forget is that when you play any game you tacitly agree to follow the rules of that game. Within the confines of those rules you cannot be "illogical or "insane" or you will "lose."

Alice learned this the hard way:

"The rule is, jam tomorrow, and jam yesterday, but never jam today."

"It must come sometimes to 'jam today,'" Alice objected.

"No, it can't," said the Queen, "It's jam every other day: today isn't any other day, you know."

(Lewis Carroll, *Through the Looking Glass*)

With this irresistible logic in mind, let's return to the seven rules of the game played at Harvard and look at them from a different point of view—not that of a student passively accepting the "inevitable" but through the eyes of a master salesperson:

1. *There are two players.* In today's complex world there are rarely just two players in any sales transaction worthy of notice. Personal preferences and judgments must be "sold" to a wide and discerning group of "buyers." The salesperson also must reverse roles,

> A skilled buyer must draw upon all corporate sources available to him or her to define objectives and needs.

seeking out experts within the company who can "sell" him on the value of goods and services that are to be offered.

2. *They play only once.* Any alert buyer will recognize this as a win-or-lose game, a gamble with high risks and no lasting benefit to either side.

3. *Each has two choices: cooperate or defect.* This choice is often encountered in "real" life. How it is handled in a sales situation often makes the difference between success and failure. (How you define success and failure also profoundly affects the outcome of a sales negotiation.)

4. *Each does not know the other's choice until the game is over.* The master salesperson always knows "where he's at" at every point in a negotiation. The only surprise should be the buyer's sudden awareness that the pie is bigger than it was when the negotiation started. Each side's share of the pie has grown proportionately.

Rules 5, 6, and 7 deal with how the smaller pie is divided. See comment on Rule 4.

Free To Win

A truism that bears repeating is that salespeople thrive on cooperation and wither away with defection. Indeed, Robert Axelrod, a professor of political science and public policy research scientist, would not set limits on this statement. He and William D. Hamilton, an evolutionary biologist, had this to say in a prize-winning article:

> Many of the benefits sought by living things are disproportionately available to cooperating groups. While there are considerable differences

in what is meant by "benefits" and "sought," this statement, insofar as it is true, lays down a fundamental basis for all social life.

("The Evolution of Cooperation," *Science* 212, no. 4489 [Mar. 27, 1981]: 1390-96.)

As with many truisms, "right thinking" human beings may agree but throw up their hands at the thought of selling it to others. First, you would have to know what fosters cooperation, and then, how to get others to cooperate. Axelrod, expanding upon the article he wrote with Hamilton, has done just that in *The Evolution of Cooperation* (New York: Basic Books, 1984).

Taking the very same "Prisoner's Dilemma" game that so bemuses the MBA students at Cambridge, he rejects the idea that it is a zerosum game: "[M]ost of life is not zero-sum. Generally, both sides can do well, or both can do poorly. Mutual cooperation is often possible, but not always achieved. That is why the Prisoner's Dilemma is such a useful model for a wide variety of everyday situations." The game is "simply an abstract formulation of some very common and very interesting situations in which what is best for each person individually leads to mutual defection, whereas everyone would have been better off with mutual cooperation." Thus, Axelrod drives a stake in the heart of Harvard's "killer instinct."

Is there any "proof" for this optimistic conclusion, or is it merely the wishful thinking of a wimp? Yes, there is "proof," and it is quite impressive.

Instead of brainwashed students competing for the approval of a dogmatic instructor (one third of their grade for the course depended on how well they played a zero-sum game), Axelrod staged a computer tournament. A number of professional game theorists were invited to submit their favorite strategy for playing the Prisoner's Dilemma game. The rules for the most part were the same as those traditionally used. (One exception was significant: Single encounters were ruled out.) Axelrod and Hamilton had agreed early on that "With two individuals destined never to meet again, the only strategy that can be called a solution to the game is to defect—always."

Accordingly, the tournament had two rounds. In the first, there were 200 moves per game. In the second, a varying, undisclosed number of moves per game minimized the "last chance" effect already noted in the Harvard game. In both rounds of the computer tournament, the simplest strategy of all those submitted "won." Not quite the Golden Rule, but close, it was called *Tit for Tat*. The winning approach was offered by Professor Anatol Rapoport.

Tit for Tat, according to Axelrod, is successful because it combines four elements of a "winning" strategy:

1. It is "nice" (because it cooperates as long as the other player does).

2. It is retaliatory (because it immediately responds to defection).

3. It is forgiving (because it is willing to cooperate again as soon as the other player does).

4. It is clear and predictable (because the other player, even a "killer," knows there is a reward for cooperation and a penalty for defection).

Despite these four elements and the fact that they all afford an infinite number of varieties of application, Tit for Tat requires only two commands: stop (defect) and go (cooperate). The strategy is to start with cooperation and thereafter do what the other player did on his or her *previous* move. Instead of attempting to anticipate your opposer's next move you convert a simple choice (cooperate or defect) into a mutual learning process that can produce a mutually rewarding result. Everybody wins.

The Rewards of Cooperating

Establishing a new discipline and seeing it accepted worldwide is surely one of the most satisfying of life's experiences. To have an authority in another field, using new data, confirm one of your major concepts is not only exciting, it compels you to take a fresh look at your original premises to see if they are still valid.

When *The Art of Negotiating*® was first published in 1968, it offered a revolutionary concept: Negotiation is not synonymous with horse trading and other zero-sum games. Instead, it is a process that, used properly, can profoundly affect human relationships and produce lasting benefits for all participants.

Despite its phenomenal effects on interpersonal, inter-organizational, and international levels, the process has by no means been unanimously accepted as a universal truth. Instead of bemoaning the perversity of humanity, which has seldom produced any noticeable change, a sales negotiator might profitably explore methods of maximizing cooperation and minimizing defection. A close look at Axelrod's computer tournament can provide helpful insights into what makes a negotiation work.

First, look at the (seemingly) dogmatic statement, "With two individuals destined never to meet again, the only strategy . . . is to defect always." Axelrod argues for this solution in game theory and in biological evolution. There is no reason to go into the reasons here. If you've ever heard a lecture on the dangers and/or rewards of a "one-night stand," you've got the idea. The risks far outweigh any possible "benefit."

This is a powerful argument for stability and against change. Unfortunately, those who use it usually view life as a series of sporadic episodes, not a continuing process. That is why "We'll meet again" is a threat to a zero-sum game player and a promise to a master salesperson.

The columnist Lou Cannon, writing in *The Washington Post* (May 21, 1984), presented "a story about a tough little Democrat, Bob Moretti, who worked hard, mastered his craft and taught Ronald Reagan much of what he knows about dealing with lawmakers." It is also the story of a masterful sales negotiator, and, if looked at from Axelrod's point of view, a way to change an "everybody loses" situation (always defect) to an "everybody wins" negotiation (use "Tit for Tat") to break the old pattern and start a new, cooperative pattern.

Moretti was speaker of the State Assembly during Reagan's second term as governor of California. Moretti's aide once described legislators as "mostly creatures of the immediate, not the important," a perfect definition of a win-or-lose game player. Reagan apparently agreed. Cannon says: "For most of his first term, Reagan had treated legislators, especially those of the opposition, as political hacks unworthy of serious attention. The Democrats, mesmerized by their own campaign rhetoric, regarded Reagan as a simpleton whose only skill was his ability to go over their heads with televised appeals to the public." The result, of course, was a stalemate.

Six months into Reagan's second term (June 1971), Moretti sent him a letter proposing "that we set aside our personal and philosophical disagreements and work to assure that the people of the state will prosper." Reagan agreed to a meeting at which Moretti told him: "Look, Governor, I don't like you particularly and I know you don't like me, but we don't have to be in love to work together. If you're serious about doing some things, then let's sit down and start doing them."

The first major result of their cooperation was the California Welfare Reform Act. In it Reagan got the reduction in welfare fraud he wanted and Moretti got increased grants for the "truly needy." A series of legislative reforms based on cooperation between the governor and the legislators followed.

Ten years later, Moretti gave Lou Cannon this explanation for the "Tit-for-Tat" cooperation that developed between the two men: "Both he and I developed a grudging respect for each other. We came from different worlds. I don't think that socially we'd ever have mixed. But when the governor gave a commitment, he kept it. And when I gave a commitment, I kept it."

Perhaps the most interesting part of Cannon's article is the fact that "Tit for Tat" was not a one-time thing for Moretti. He regarded it as an essential strategy in a continuing process of negotiating with the governor. For example, in 1973 Reagan tried to limit state tax revenues with a ballot proposition. Although polls showed that the proposition had overwhelming public support, Moretti considered it unfair to the poor people of the state. He defected, led a lonely fight against the proposition, and got it defeated. Did the Reagan camp retaliate? Quite the contrary. They showed they could play "Tit for Tat" as well as Moretti. After their defection was met by Moretti's, both sides returned to cooperation. Michael K. Deaver, who managed the losing campaign, said, "Bob had the guts to take us on when the other Democrats wouldn't, and he won. He was a good winner . . . and when he lost, he was also a good loser. He was a professional in the best sense of the word."

Establishing a Cooperative Climate

Deaver's comment on winners and losers reveals a basic philosophical difference between the Reaganauts and Moretti. The first group apparently viewed the relationship as a series of discrete games, some of which you win and some you lose. *How* you play the game (what tactics you use) is more important than your score in each game. (After all, it is a zero-sum game.) Moretti played an entirely different game, one with an unlimited number of plays and a cumulative score that could convince both sides that

> Tactics are important in that you want to play each game as well as possible.

they were winners. However, strategies are paramount in establishing long-range goals. As a salesperson, you are not interested in a one-night stand, you want to initiate the negotiating process. You want to exchange ideas with others aimed at changing your relationship with them. You want to reach agreements that benefit both of you and pave the way for future agreements.

In a "perfect" world, both you and the buyer would always cooperate and both of you would soon be out of a job. Who would need you? In a less-than-perfect world, both of you might choose to defect always, with the same results as before. In the "real" world you would identify your personal and organizational needs and those of the buyer. Then you would try to negotiate a settlement that would bring maximum benefits to both of you. But what if the buyer wants to "win" big and defects? Can you, as a salesperson, "afford" to defect? This is a question I often have been asked (and, I must confess, I often have asked myself). Remembering that Axelrod calls the "Prisoner's Dilemma" game simply an abstract formulation for some very common and interesting situations, it might be better to ask yourself if you can afford not to defect? You certainly don't want to perpetuate a situation where you are always the "sucker." Your objective is to change the relationship so both of you can "win." Tit for Tat, an "abstract formulation," works very well as a strategy in computer tournaments. Implementing it with *The Art of Negotiating®* tactics, you can come up with two sure winners in real-life sales negotiations.

When you begin to implement your sales strategy with negotiating tactics, always keep in mind that game playing usually limits you to two choices: yes or no, cooperate or defect, hit or miss, win or lose. In real life even an infant has many more alternatives than that.

> Negotiations are seldom "called on account of darkness," but games may be. In game playing, tactics are often subject to arbitrary time limits. In the negotiating process, time is used to achieve change. You achieve your objective in your "own good time."

How and where you play a game is also determined by arbitrary rules. In negotiation, you set your own limits. That is why "Tit for Tat" is a "nice" strategy. You do not limit your opposer's options to act in any way she chooses. However, you do impose limits on yourself as to how far and where you will go in achieving a negotiated solution. Your goal is to change your relationship with your opposer, not to change yourself just to be accommodating. The New Testament question is still relevant today: "For what is a man profited, if he shall gain the whole world, and lose his own soul?"

The "Right" Way to Defect

Defection should not be an either/or matter. Blowing an opposer's ship out of the water may win a battle, but it's a poor tactic to use when you want to get a sales contract. You may blame your response on "human nature," but the real villain is a zero-sum game that both of you have played once and lost. If you had used your defection not as a weapon but as you would a tugboat, you might have nudged your opposer into calmer waters where cooperation could flourish.

An example of waiting too long took place in Pittsburgh in June 1984. A retired couple living on a limited pension won the right to evict their 43-year-old son and to collect for three years of back rent and utility bills. The son, who had a good job, stopped paying expenses when the couple increased his monthly payments to $200. His mother took him to court twice and won. The son appealed both times but lost for the third time after a jury had deliberated 10 minutes.

Asked why she had waited so long to act, the mother, obviously slow to anger, said, "I spoiled the hell out of him. It just took me a while to realize he's nothing but a chiseler." It would be nice to report that this poor, put-upon mother lived happily ever after, but it is doubtful. She said of her son, "I hate to say this, but he doesn't exist. I've replaced him. I got a puppy." If she had used cooperation and then tit for tat at a very early stage the story might have been different. Sometimes it is better to negotiate with the old dog you know than with an unpredictable puppy.

As a salesperson you, of course, want to establish a cooperative climate that enables everybody to win. Once in a great while you can establish an instant rapport and make an *"easy"* sale. If that were the end of it, you might consider yourself fortunate. However, if you consider negotiation a process, you might very well see defection and a return to cooperation during negotiation preferable to defection *after* the negotiation has "ended." Return counters are a constant

> Once you accept the concept that negotiating is a process, defection becomes not only thinkable but even desirable.

reminder of that "truth." Successful sales negotiations seldom have a formal ending. That comes only when both sides always defect. Edward L. Bernays, "The Father of Public Relations," reminiscing at age 92 about his distinguished career, provides these insights into the use of defection in negotiation:

> One day in 1934 George Washington Hill told me he was losing half the cigarette market because men wouldn't let women smoke on the street. I went to a psychoanalyst and asked him what smoking meant to women. "It's a torch of freedom," he told me, "a symbol of man's inhumanity to women. It also titillates the erogenous zone of the lips."

> So that Easter I called up some debs I knew, and they got their pictures in the papers for the Easter Parade on Boston Common, Central Park, places like that. Smoking. Within three days the *Times* reported women were smoking in public in four major cities. Five weeks later the New York theaters lifted the ban on women smoking in the orchestra-pit smoking stalls they had then.

The *tactic* Bernays used was Association, linking the "beautiful people" with a "chic" habit. The *strategy* used was Disassociation, a defection from traditional social customs.

There is a sequel to the story. Long after Bernays had successfully sold the public on equal rights in smoking, he became persuaded that smoking can cause cancer. He defected from the tobacco companies, ending that relationship, and began a new negotiation, this time cooperating with the anti-tobacco forces. One of the tactics his firm used was Blanketing. The firm was a major factor in banning cigarette ads on radio and television. The First Amendment made such a ban impossible to apply to the press, so less effective ammunition, such as "warnings," was used. Bernays' second defection was perhaps less effective than the first because it was selling "denial" rather than "freedom," but it exacted a toll.

Negotiation, like life, is not a game, but as the above story indicates, "Tit for Tat" can be an effective negotiating tool. The difference is that in the Prisoner's Dilemma game you deal with one opposer at a time. No successful salesperson does that in "real" life. When you defect from one participant you do so by cooperating with another person and/or adopting another point of view with the aim of changing your relationship with the buyer. If you feel inadequate to deal with an experienced buyer in a highly technical field, you must find experts within your own company and cooperate with them. In that way you can identify your problem and devise tactics to deal with it.

One word of warning: You can never learn too much about the product you want to sell but you can never learn it all. You must establish a bridge of cooperation between your company and a potential buyer.

> Remember that your job is not to make the product but to sell it.

Sooner or later, the buyer is going to defect. What then? The amateur salesperson does not retaliate and defect. He throws in the towel because he cannot exist in an uncooperative world. The master salesperson defects, because although he or she is aware of his or her own and his or her company's needs, he or she obviously does not know enough about his or her opposers. To discover them he or she must defect, adopt new tactics to deal with the new situation, and bring the negotiating process back on course. Then cooperation can resume.

Key Points

This chapter provided you with the understanding of alternatives, and the choices you are able to make in your life. From all recent studies, it appears that cooperation offers you the best rewards.

What Happened to the Bacon? Only Time Will Tell

13

What Happened to the Bacon? Only Time Will Tell

"A wise man makes more opportunity than he finds."

Francis Bacon, *"Of Ceremonies and Respects,"* Essays,
1625

"There is no security on earth. There is only opportunity."

Douglas MacArthur, quoted in Courtney Whitney's,
His Rendezvous with History, 1955

In the good old days, when Chicago was "Hog Butcher for the World," meat packers boasted that they were able to sell everything except the pig's squeal. On a hot summer day when the wind was blowing right, old-timers agreed that every other by-product of the process had its price and sometimes exacted a heavy toll. Today, the squeals, the smells, the pigs, and the packers all are gone. The Willy Lomans lament the loss of this efficient, centralized operation: Pigs went in, pork came out. All you had to do was sell it. After all, as an American philosopher once said: "Pigs is pigs."

Edward Bernays, master negotiator, reminiscing on his career in Public relations, at least made it sound easy: "Beechnut Packing was having trouble selling bacon. They came to me, and it occurred to me that maybe Americans weren't eating enough breakfast. So we polled 5,000 doctors, and they said, 'Yes, a person needs a good big breakfast to get through the day. Like bacon and eggs.' Bacon sales went up overnight."

From another point of view it wasn't that easy. A laying hen and a pig were once admiring a billboard featuring a platter of bacon and eggs. "See," the hen said, "We're partners."

"That's easy enough for you to say," the pig replied. "For you it's a day's work. For me it's a lifetime dedication."

Make Time Your Ally

Dedication and hard work have always been regarded as essential attributes of amateur, competent, and master salespeople alike. How to explain the wide disparity of results among them? Certainly the way they regard and use time is a major factor. Amateurs often are victims of time because they do not understand its proper use. They enter a time warp and refuse to admit the possibility of change. The "good old days" (no matter how bad they actually were) are always preferable to the present. Competent salespersons are opportunists and gamblers. They make a move when they feel that their opposers are vulnerable and are likely losers. Master salespersons make time an ally in their negotiating process. They realize that time inevitably creates change—new needs to be met, and new opportunities to reach mutually satisfying agreements with buyers.

The Bernays bacon-and-egg story is a good example of a master salesperson using time as an ally. It should be conceded that a cynic today might call him an opportunist. Where on earth would you find 5,000 doctors today recommending a hearty breakfast of bacon and eggs? But Bernays was not a clairvoyant. He recognized that time had changed the eating habits of American city dwellers. Farm workers still fortified themselves with incredible breakfasts, but office workers had neither the time nor the inclination to bother much with breakfast. Bernays was smart enough to spot the trend and supply the inclination: Good breakfasts meant good health. Bacon and eggs constituted a "good" breakfast. The doctors told him they did.

In time, of course, other food manufacturers jumped on the bandwagon. Brand X cereals, for example, were an essential part of a "good" breakfast. Later, cereals were "less" fattening than bacon and eggs. Then cholesterol reared its ugly head and with it the possible threat of arteriosclerosis. Bacon had "lots" of cholesterol. Other foods had "less" cholesterol or, even "better," had polyunsaturated oils or fats.

Each of these changes wrought by time brought new challenges and new opportunities to salespeople on all levels. Amateurs would seek out the "true believers" (there are always some left) to win a piece of an ever-shrinking pie. Competent salespeople would learn a new pitch and try to cash in on an innovation. Master salespeople, acting as a bridge between the maker of a product and the buyer, created new markets out of the changes that time had brought about. In time they may even find a market for the squeal.

Where's The Bacon?

A modern-day Rig van Winkle returning to Chicago after a 30-year sleep would be baffled not only by the disappearance of the Union Stock Yards but by the apparent demise of our once-famous meat packers. Many of them seem to have vanished without a trace. A quick course in diversification and conglomeration might clear up some of the ambiguities, but it still would be hard to explain where the bacon is.

Time hid some of the many errors of consolidation of the past. The great merger mania that swept the United States in the 1960s was based on a perceived need to correct the supposed "errors" of the past. How this was to be done, how conglomeration was to be "sold," can be seen in an article by Leslie Wayne (The *New York Times*, Nov. 15, 1981). By the time the article was published, the "errors of the past" were those of conglomeration.

Wayne's list of its then current drawbacks clearly reveals the assumptions on which the urge to merge was based:

1. Diversified companies do not necessarily fare better during an economic slump.

2. Skilled executives in one line of business frequently are unable to apply their specialized knowledge to unrelated businesses.

3. Conglomerate stocks, after initial investor enthusiasm, have become a "drug" on the market.

4. Division managers are insulated from the consequences of make-or-break decisions by layers of management over them. This encourages a feeling that "The most I can lose is my job."

5. Top management is beginning to look beyond the assumed advantages of the conglomerate to the rate of return on their investment in individual divisions. Often the better choice is investment in new businesses, in different divisions within the conglomerate, or in financial securities.

How Good is "Desperately Anxious"?

These sober second thoughts after years of unbridled growth left many conglomerate divisions in a state of suspended animation, waiting for the blow to fall.

Wayne detailed the next step:

"When the decision is made to shed a company, the conglomerate faces several alternatives. It can liquidate it. It can sell it to another company. Or it can sell it to the executives running it." While buy-outs by management increased dramatically in the late 1970s, details of these generally private transactions were hard to come by. Usually, only participating investment firms and the management knew for sure what the intricate details of the financial package were. There was one "given," however. As a close observer said: "Investors want management to go in up to their eyeballs. They want management to be committed, desperately anxious. . . . They tell management, 'If it works, you'll be rich, and if it fails, I won't be alone.'"

The master salesperson can't help feeling a certain bemusement at this bit of meta-talk. Is desperate anxiety conducive to business

> In a successful negotiation, everybody wins.

success? Here there seems to be one potential winner (management) against two potential losers (management and investor). It is reminiscent of jungle warfare or a trip on the Titanic. The only possible "winner" is management, which would then become rich. Somehow this seems a rather meager result for a deal involving millions.

Leveraged Buyouts

Despite George Orwell's dire predictions, when 1984 rolled by, no Big Brother was in sight. Predictably, however, an old fad under a new name dominated the buyer's market. The old name, "bootstrap financing," conjured up a distasteful picture of hard labor and meager rewards. In 1984 Newspeak, the old process was renamed "leveraged buyout." The patron saint of the movement was William E. Simon, a former Treasury Secretary. Simon and a partner obtained Gibson Greeting Cards from RCA in a leveraged buyout. After taking it private, they later took it public. Simon netted about $70 million on his original investment of $300,000. Daniel F. Cuff, in an article entitled "Perils of Leveraged Buyouts" (The *New York Times*, May 14, 1984), presented some good news and some bad news about such buyouts:

> So far, leveraged buyouts—the purchase of a company by a group of investors and financed mainly by borrowing against the assets of the company—have generally led only to great success for the participants and investors.

> But there are increasing warnings from bankers and other providers of funds that the game is getting too risky. Insurance companies, pension funds and big credit companies say that prices have been bid too high and that the economics of

many of the deals are not acceptable. An economic downturn or higher interest rates could threaten some companies highly leveraged with debt.

An old Latin warning, *caveat emptor* (Let the buyer beware), seems appropriate here. Once large sums of money are involved in a "game," somebody's going to lose. By coincidence, three weeks after Cuff's article appeared, Dean Witter Reynolds Inc. announced that it had filed a registration statement with the Securities and Exchange Commission to begin marketing the first leveraged buyout fund available for individual investors. The closed-end investment fund would be managed by the Equus Capital Corporation. Investors would become limited partners. The funds raised would be used to finance the equity portions of leveraged buyouts. When the companies involved were sold, the resulting capital gains, *if there were any* (author's italics), would be distributed, with the general partner receiving the customary 20 percent and the limited partners 80 percent. (By the way, *equus* is the Latin word for *horse*.)

Win-Win vs. Everybody Wins

The preceding examples of merger mania, buyouts by management, and leveraged buyouts show that no matter how timely each appeared when it came on the economic scene, none had a life span longer than a pig's, The "movers and shakers" in these deals felt that life was a game, and they wanted to win big. Possibly they did, but their triumphs did not last long.

Many students of the negotiating process have tried to analyze negotiating skills in strict accordance with John von Neumann and Oskar Morgenstem's Theory of Games and Economic Behavior. They forget that the creators of game theory stated that life is not a game. Games have a finite number of variables, whereas life offers unlimited choices. The value structure of a game is accepted by the players, whereas life situations are unstructured. Game theory has a possible use in preparing for a negotiation because it can stimulate thought and suggest creative alternatives, but it cannot impose arbitrary game limits upon the negotiating process.

It is also a mistake to compare the negotiation process to a game in which both sides win. The ideal results of a negotiation is not the win/win choice of the game theory but rather the Everybody Wins® theory of life. If the two participants in a sales negotiation both win but the third participant, the public, loses, you have not created a stable negotiation outcome.

For example, Cuff says: "One favored aspect of the leveraged buyout is tax treatment. Newly bought-out companies usually can take more depreciation deductions, and the interest on the borrowed money, in contrast to dividends, is deductible." He quotes an expert "There has never been a leveraged buyout that was not tax-oriented."

A footnote: Kohlberg, Kravis, Roberts & Company has been very successful in arranging some of the largest leveraged buyouts. Its most ambitious proposal was to make a private company out of Esmark, Inc., a Midwest holding company, at the cost of $2.4 billion. Not familiar with the name? It grew out of the old Swift meatpacking company. Somewhere along the line, Swift sold the pig, squeal and all, and instead of Swift, a stranger is bringing home the bacon.

Key Points

Master sales negotiators use time as an ally. They do not regard change as a threat but as an opportunity to grow and sell more successfully.

One of the best ways of finding new sales opportunities is to examine the assumptions that make up the conventional wisdom of the moment. Changing your point of view by seeing the flaws in the assumptions will permit you to change and/or improve the product you are selling.

Merger mania, buyouts by management, and leveraged buyouts have all provided short-lived excitement. Can you recognize successful future programs before they explode like fireworks? The Master Negotiator will check them against Win Lose, Win Win, and Everybody Wins. Only when everybody wins can there be any permanence.

What It Takes
To Be Heard

What It Takes To Be Heard

"A smooth sea new made a skillful mariner."

English Proverb

In 1982 the columnist and humorist, Russell Baker, was bemused by some calculations he had made. He reckoned that Edward Gibbon had required 1,170 printed pages for his *Decline and Fall of the Roman Empire*, whereas Henry A. Kissinger needed 1,283 pages for the first volume of his memoirs, which covered 0.15 percent of the time span that Gibbon had dealt with in his work. The reason for this difference is not hard to find. Kissinger was a negotiator intimately involve in great affairs of state, while Gibbon was a distant, fairly objective observer. Experienced negotiators are well aware of the problem.

Even a relatively straightforward negotiation between two individuals is bound to involve conflicting interests and loyalties, different levels of needs and varying strategies for reaching an agreement. Transferred from a private conference room to a world stage, each factor is magnified (and possibly distorted) to suit the convictions and predilections of each observer and participant, and the story becomes longer.

Once in a great while, the general public perceives a negotiator as having "star quality." He or she is a "winner" at solving any problem, and the public wants to know exactly how it is done. This was certainly true of Kissinger, and his account of his triumphs, occasionally interspersed with stories of big ones that got away, probably will resist the onslaughts of revisionist historians for some time. One thing seems fairly certain: If or when a historian succeeds in downgrading Kissinger, it will not be because his negotiating techniques were wrong but because the policies they implemented are suddenly seen as failures. Gibbon, after all, did not write "The Rise and Triumph of the Roman Empire"— that had been done countless times before. Instead he viewed the story as he might a well-made play, with a beginning, a middle, and an end. He wrote the end of the story.

Communication Should Work Both Ways

All too often we think of negotiation as an event, preferably one where everyone lives happily ever after. If we are realistic, we think of it as a process and remember Leroy (Satchel) Paige's admonition: "Let whosoever wishes sit around recollecting. I'm looking up the line."

This is a good philosophy to adopt when you are attempting to realize the full benefits you have gained from a successful negotiation. However, a backward look at sales opportunities you missed or negotiations in which you failed can help you prepare for future efforts.

Many sales negotiations fail to achieve maximum benefits for both sides because the salesperson fails as a communicator. Most of the time it is a sin of omission—the "right" information is not presented clearly and positively. More rarely it is a sin of commission—the "wrong" information is presented.

As a result, one horrible example of this took place in Geneva, Switzerland, in 1982. An article by Leslie H. Gelb (*New York Times*, May 2, 1982) on the resumption of the U.S.-U.S.S.R. strategic arms limitation talks reviewed the issues involved and the competing interests inside the U.S. government that were attempting to shape negotiating strategies. Whether these strategies were used when the talks opened almost two months later is less important than the fact that they were seriously considered. Two items stand out in the evaluation of possible opening moves:

The first: "The main burden of the new (U.S.) approach would fall on the Soviet Union, which would have to reduce, if not eliminate, its force of large land-based missiles with multiple warheads."

The second: "Administration analysts were told not even to consider the acceptability of any new plan to Moscow, just to lay out what was best for the United States and let Moscow make a counter-offer."

The first assumes that the "only" way to open a negotiation is by stating a maximum position. The opposer, in this case the U.S.S.R., would have to accept the terms, no matter how distasteful, and forgo any advantages that might accrue from its present strengths. Most experienced negotiators would be hard pressed to find such an accommodating opponent.

The next item seems at first glance to be another statement of a maximum position. Actually it was much more—potentially more damaging than an ultimatum. Essentially it was a wish list of "what was best for the United States." As such it imposed limits on the United States, *not* on the U.S.S.R

When you present your opposer with a list of everything you think you could possibly want and let him pick and choose what he is willing to give you, you are viewing negotiation as you might a letter to Santa Claus. You fail to consider the all-important needs and reactions of your opposer in structuring your position. You take what is offered to you. You let your opposer do your work for you, and you suffer the consequences. Remember that Faust thought he had a great deal until he realized that his pact with Satan was a process, not a happy event.

Gobbledygook

A federal judge yesterday ordered the government to rewrite Medicare benefit form letters in plain English, saying their "bureaucratic gobbledygook" defies understanding.

U.S. District Court Judge Jack B. Weinstein of Brooklyn said that when certain Medicare recipients challenge their payments, they receive letters that are "incomprehensible" and "misleading." "The language used is bureaucratic gobbledygook, jargon, double talk, a form of officialese, federalese and insurancese and doublespeak," Weinstein wrote. "It does not qualify as English." The decision came in a class-action suit filed on behalf of thousands of Medicare recipients in Queens against the federal government and Group Health Inc., which administers part of the program in the New York borough.

Phrases such as "approved charges," "prevailing charges," "economic index," and "physicians' old and new profile," which are the substance of the letter, are specialized Medicare vocabulary, he said."To a layman unfamiliar with Medicare regulations, this language has no real meaning," the judge said. *Washington Post*, July 8, 1984.

Usually I go along with Voltaire: "I disapprove of what you say, but I will defend to the death your right to say it." When I don't understand what you say, however, I am reluctant to give my approval or disapproval.

Many salespeople, especially those breaking into a new field, feel they are handicapped because they are not masters of a specialized vocabulary. (Cynics might call it *gobbledygook*.) Certainly it is an advantage if you and the buyer "speak the same language," but there are potential problems as well. A major one is that you cannot be absolutely sure that you and the buyer are in mutual agreement on the "true" meaning of each and every specialized phrase. This uncertainty can make you the victim of your own false assumptions. Certainly it has been a bonanza for many an unscrupulous negotiator.

Use of gobbledygook is a luxury no salesperson can afford. It may save time but it also may cost you a lot. Remember that the buyer is not the only person you are negotiating with. Even if both of you are in perfect accord on what you have said, there are many others—people in your company, people in the buyer's organization, and interested outsiders—who must also be "sold." See Judge Weinstein's comments above.

Use Questions Wisely

Another disadvantage of gobbledygook is that it inhibits the use of questions, that most valuable tool of the sales negotiator. Because "everybody" knows in advance what the "truth" is, why ask. Amateur salespeople are often reluctant to ask questions because they are afraid they will betray ignorance. Well, ignorance is always there at the start of a negotiation, whether the person is an amateur or a master negotiator. What are your opposer's needs? You find out by asking questions. How do you proceed with the negotiation?

> The proper use of questions will guide you. Circumstances will control your decisions on what questions to ask, how to phrase them, and when to ask them.

Of course, you want to ask questions that provide information that is useful to you, but you also want them to stimulate your opposer's thoughts. General questions should be avoided. The *New York Post*, July 6, 1984, provides an example: "Nigeria's ambassador was called to the British foreign office to explain why one of his aides was at Stansted Airport supervising the loading of 'diplomatic' crates containing former Nigerian Transport Minister Urnaru Dikko and two other Nigerian exiles." The ambassador's thoughts certainly must have been stimulated, but we doubt that much useful information was obtained. "What's going on here?" just won't get the facts you need.

As a lawyer, you are permitted to use questions to control testimony. By asking specific questions, you can even guide and control the thoughts of the other party. Former Congressman, Jurist,and trial lawyer Louis Heller provides this example:

> Q. When you say you don't remember, Mr. Jones, do you mean by that that you remembered it and forgot it, or that you never remembered it at all?

> A. I remembered it and forgot it.

> Q. Your accident happened on January 10, 1948, and today is March14, 1953. I know that you cannot give me the exact date that you forgot it, but you certainly can give me the year?

> A. It was in 1952.

> Q. Thank you for your assistance. Now that you remember that you forgot it in 1952, I know that you forgot it, but can you tell me what time of year it was?

> A. Some time in the middle of the year.

> Q. Would it be a fair statement that it was some time between June and August? Is that what you mean by the middle of the year?

> A. Yes, sir.

Q. I know you don't remember the precise time of day that you forgot it. I am sure, however, that you can tell us whether it was early morning, afternoon, or evening.

A. It was some time in the afternoon.

Q. From your answer, I take it that you forgot it in the year 1952, sometime between June and August and during the afternoon? Is that right?

A. Yes, sir.

The moral of this story is that if you regard sales negotiation correctly—that is, as a process rather than as a win-or-lose game—you will use questions to understand and advance the process. You may even gather up some meaningful "truths" along the way.

Putting Yourself in the Other's Shoes

People involved in negotiation of necessity must try to put themselves in the other's position to discover their opposers' needs, points of view, qualifications, and many other bits of information that will advance the negotiation. If this effort results in an everybody wins negotiation, fine. If it doesn't, who's to blame? Experience shows that the salesperson will usually get the blame (from the buyer) if the buyer is the loser, and none of the praise if the buyer wins. This often happens when the buyer reverses roles and puts himself in the salesperson's shoes.

Paul W. Valentine (*Washington Post*, July 19, 1984) provides an interesting example:

"When . . . a suburban Baltimore attorney bought his glossy white, fully loaded 1976 Cadillac Eldorado convertible in August 1976 for $16,250, he thought he had made a smart move." His reason? Between 1965, when America's infatuation with convertibles peaked, and 1971, when the bottom began to drop out of the market, General Motors thought it had seen the wave of the future. In 1976 it pushed that year's model as "the last convertible in America" and "a priceless collector's item." The attorney bought the sales pitch and paid $5,201 over list price for his treasure. He thought he was getting a bargain because some people were paying $20,000 or more for the same model.

"Some collectors kept their convertibles, undriven, in undisclosed garages. Others hired security guards to protect their prizes. GM offered the very last convertible to the Smithsonian Institution but was turned down." The attorney drove his car "back and forth to the beach," running up about 30,000 miles between 1976 and late 1983. By then convertibles were back on the market. GM's Pontiac started the renewed trend and was soon followed by Cadillac and others.

What did the attorney, buyer, and would-be salesperson do? With a chiropractor and fellow "victim" he sued GM, demanding that the company compensate some 14,000 purchasers of the 1976 model for alleged monetary losses. No matter who "won," everybody lost.

> If you are going to slip into someone else's shoes, make sure they fit.

A Checklist For Evaluating Your Sales and Buying Negotiating Skills

1. Are you aware of when your negotiation starts?
2. Do you know the issues to be negotiated?
3. Do you make an effort to create a negotiating climate?

4. Do you listen actively?

5. Do you feel that you can change a person's attitude in relation to yourself?

6. Do you use questions and allow a sufficient time for them to be answered?

7. Do you try to use many alternatives to negotiating?

8. Do you recapitulate for greater comprehension and understanding?

9. Do you make an effort to overcome semantic difficulties or technical language?

10. Do you know the risks of disclosure and when and how to use disclosure?

11. Are you separating fact-finding from negotiating?

12. Are you avoiding creating limits too quickly?

13. Are you avoiding closing doors on other alternatives?

14. Do you know how to use concessions for effective sales negotiating?

A master negotiator would answer the above questions positively.

Key Points

Sales negotiations are not fairy tales with a happy ending. Indeed, successful sales seldom have happy endings. They are the beginning of a process that is good for a lifetime.

This chapter has a checklist for evaluating your negotiating skills. Many other evaluations will be presented to help you integrate these into your negotiating "personality" as you proceed:

- Know what you need to know to be heard.
- Stop using gobbledygook.
- Questions have many functions. Use them wisely.
- Learn to put yourself in the other's shoes.

Negotiation Skills in Everyday Life

Negotiation Skills in Everyday Life

"*The winds and the waves are always on the side of the ablest navigators.*"

Edward Gibbon, Decline and Fall of the Roman Empire,
1776

In our study of the Art of Negotiating® we have examined the philosophy and psychology behind negotiating strategy and have learned how to prepare for negotiations. We have considered human behavior, as it relates to both negotiation and fundamental human needs. We have developed the *Need Theory*—simply a matter of recognizing needs by asking questions and developing a negotiating strategy that will meet the paramount needs of both parties as fully as possible.

Negotiation is a tool for influencing human behavior—a tool that can be used effectively by anyone. It's not some specialized skill suitable for use only by professionals. Negotiation is an art that is closely allied to all kinds of human activities. I will use and have used examples from the business world to demonstrate how to be a master negotiator in buy/sell situations, but negotiating plays an important role in all our relations. You probably use it to get the youngsters to take out the garbage. You might negotiate with your spouse to determine how much of your paycheck goes toward household expenses.

Master negotiators must combine the alertness and speed of an expert swordsman with the sensitivity of an artist. They must be ready to spot any loopholes in the opposers' positions, and any shifts in their strategies. At the correct moment, they must select from their palette of options exactly the right combination of action and inaction, forcefulness and withdrawal to establish balanced relationships, in which everybody wins.

I hope it has become abundantly clear that success in negotiation does not necessarily mean getting your own way all the time. Successful negotiation is essentially a matter of sensitivity and good timing. You want to build mutually beneficial, supportive relationships. In our personal lives, as in business, what goes around comes around.

It was not my intention to cover the vast spectrum of negotiations possible in everyday living. This book was intended to mainly help you in a business context. But it's important to realize that our business lives cannot be completely divorced from our personal lives. The personality traits and interpersonal strengths and weaknesses we develop in each arena will carry over into the other. Whether in a personal relationship or a commercial transaction, you should be able to recognize those situations where the name is "negotiate."

Final Hints and Advice for the Master Negotiator

16

Final Hints and Advice for the Master Negotiator

16

A knowledge of negotiation will bring you your greatest rewards.

Therefore, review these 20 important elements in the negotiating process.

1. Understand that negotiation is a process. It's a changing process, and the master negotiator must always be alert to changes.

> Remember that negotiation occurs whenever two people meet with the intention of changing their relationship.

2. Take advantage of the fact that during a negotiating process, you will receive feedback (changes in the process) and be able to deal with it and move forward. You can and will make your future happen.

3. Recognize that negotiation is a cooperative process, and you can bring about more permanent results when every one cooperates to achieve those results. This can be accomplished by understanding the difference among win-or-lose, win-and-win, and Everybody Wins®. In Everybody Wins®, you take into account the conclusions that will allow more permanent results.

4. Prepare alternatives. Alternative creative thinking is always available and improves negotiation performance.

5. Know yourself and others. Understanding conceptions and misconceptions of human nature are essential skills.

> Avoid rigid, commonly accepted views of other cultures, societies, or individuals.

6. Prepare for the negotiation.

   a. Work to understand the mutuality of the subject matter.

   b. Know the objectives.

   c. Know the issues.

   d. Know the positions.

   e. Develop the team. Understand its composition and individual requirements.

   f. Select a site for the negotiation carefully. It can help create the type of climate you need. The site should be determined after reviewing all considerations involved in the negotiation.

   g. Review, wherever possible, the previous negotiating results involving the parties.

   h. Prepare your choices of openings and closings. Be certain you have your closing position in which you ask for what you want, need, or desire.

7. Discover the facts. Difficulties with fact-finding can be resolved by understanding that your assumptions are made before you develop your facts. It should be considered a separate stage, in which both sides review their assumptions and try to bring about some agreement on the assumptions and the facts, rather than resorting to arguments.

8. Operate under the Nierenberg Need Theory, in which the satisfaction of the needs of all parties are considered. This theory deals with the general needs of all human beings.

9   Avoid these common reasons for negotiating failure:

   a. No planning, no long-range objectives, and inappropriate short-range objectives.

   b. Emotional barriers, misunderstanding negotiating logic and misconception of what is common sense, and irrational behavior.

10. Map your strategies and tactics and the way in which they should be used as valid methods to achieve long-term satisfactory results. They should be divided simply into timing and how-and-where strategies and tactics, which help to move the negotiating process.

11. Study and practice the Negotiation Efficiency Guide:

   a. Not too much

   b. Not too little

   c. Be effective

   d. Gain heart with trusting climates

   e. Gain ear with your rhetoric

   f. Gain mind with your logic

   g. Gain eyes with your elegance

   h. Gain a soulmate through The Art of Negotiation®

12. Understand that questions in a negotiation move the process step by step. Do not use questions to manipulate.

13 .Negotiate climates. You are the creator of the emotional environments, and there are almost unlimited amounts of climates you can create.

> Maintaining a positive climate brings about positive results.

14. Observe the levels of negotiating. Never feel blocked in seeking a negotiation solution. By changing levels, you can involve a new and different group of individuals with different needs. Here are some elements of dealing with changing levels:

    a. Negotiating between individuals

    b. Negotiating within a group

    c. Negotiating with groups

    d. Negotiating within an organization

    e. Negotiating between organizations

    f. Negotiating within a nation

    g. Negotiating between nations

15. Live with agreements. The end results are not only the gains that you may have achieved from the negotiation but also your ability to continue the relationship with your agreement. You should seek stable results, not unresolved conclusions or seeds for future problems.

16. Test the final agreement.

    a. Is it livable, permanent, and stable?

    b. Is it salable to people outside the negotiation who have an interest in the results?

    c. Are the results unpredictable because the conclusions are unknown and unstable?

17. Analyze the loss of your negotiating opportunities.

    a. What were the methods you used?

    b. What were the purposes involved?

    c. Make a checklist of what you learned from this lost opportunity.

    d. How can it be avoided in the future?

18 Be aware of *sub-rosa* negotiating signs and signals. These are verbal and nonverbal. These signals should be looked for before the negotiation starts, while it is going on, and when it is supposedly concluded. These signals should be used to appreciate the feelings of the other side and enable you to accommodate their feelings.

19 Be alert to what is happening in research on the negotiation process. We are still in the stages of understanding more and more about it.

20. Develop a philosophy of negotiation. It's most important to understand that your negotiation philosophy influences your results. If you are not satisfied with your results and you feel you can change, try Everybody Wins®. I have found that this philosophy brings the greatest results to all. It has positive effects on all, yourself, and the opposer.

Step-by-Step Negotiation Preparation

Step-by-Step Negotiation Preparation

17

"Doing business without advertising is like winking at someone in the dark. You know what you're doing but nobody else does."

Steuart Hendemon Britt, *New York Herald Tribune*, Oct. 30, 1956

Although each negotiation is an individual event, the necessary preparation remains the same for all negotiations. The following pages will take you through the preparation for a negotiation step by step. For the purposes of this exercise, choose a negotiation you will be involved in or one you have already completed. Throughout the process, keep a note pad handy. Write down any questions or comments you might have for further consideration.

The Computer As Coach

This exercise is abstracted from *The Art of Negotiating®* Software preparation program produced by Experience in Software, Inc., 2000 Hearst Avenue, Berkeley, CA 94709; 800-678-7008. www.projectkickstart.com.

Running this program on a computer will provide many added dimensions for individual and team preparation, such as printing out all the materials to be used for the negotiation, an agenda, and the latest in group preparation methods.

Section I: Subject Matter

Your first step is to identify who will be involved in the negotiation and what the negotiation will be about.

Who is negotiating?

1. Your name: _____

2. Name of organization you're negotiating for: _____

_____

3. Name of anyone else on your side: _____

_____

Note: If you're part of a negotiating team, be sure to answer the questions in Section II.

4. Name of person on the other side: _____

5. Name of the organization: _____

6. Name of any additional people who might appear on the opposer's side: _____

_____

7 Are there people who aren't directly involved with your negotiation, but who may influence or be influenced by its outcome?

Party: Influence:

_____   _____

_____   _____

_____   _____

8. Find any information possible about your opposer's previous negotiations.

a. Are there any patterns? _____

b. What techniques were used? _____

c. Who made the final decisions? _____

What is this negotiation about?

1. Check one topic that best depicts the area under negotiation:

☐ Litigation ☐ Enforcement

☐ Real Estate ☐ Franchise

☐ Mergers/acquisitions/divestitures

☐ Personnel ☐ Interpersonal relationships

☐ Other _____

2. State the subject matter in one line or less. _____

_____

3. Write a sentence that you feel reflects your opposer's description of the subject matter. _____

_____

_____

4. Do the two sides agree? If not, write a sentence that defines the subject matter in a way that is agreeable to both sides. _____

_____

_____

Section II: The Negotiation Team

Here are some questions to consider when you are setting up a negotiating team.

1. How many people will be on the team? _____

2. What professionals/experts do you need to support your points?_____

3. Make a list of the people who will be on your team, and note what information or function each will be responsible for.

Name   Responsibility

_____   _____

_____   _____

_____   _____

_____   _____

4. Is everyone clear on the objectives and issues of the negotiation?

5. How will everyone participate?

   ❑ Assigned topics   ❑   Taking turns

   ❑ Open discussion   ❑   Other _____

6. What prearranged signals will you use to tell each other to stop talking? _____

   Change the subject? _____

   Change the strategy? _____

   Other: _____

7. Have you taken advantage of group creative approaches to the negotiation, such as The Idea Generator® Plus, an additional software program, also produced by Experience in Software?

Section III: Objectives

Objectives are the desired results of a negotiation. For example, one side might be looking for a 15 percent pay increase while the other side wants a 20 percent growth in sales. Both sides usually have many objectives. You should be familiar with all of your objectives in a given negotiation, and you should anticipate your opposer's objectives. The better prepared you are in this regard, the more likely you are to be successful.

In the following chart:

- List your objectives

- List your opposer's objectives

- Check off any of your objectives that conflict with those of your opposer

- Check off any objectives your opposer has that conflict with yours

- Rate your objectives according to their importance: 9 = very important; 1 = not important
- Do the same for your opposer's objectives

You now have a foundation for your negotiation. Conflicting objectives will determine the issues to be discussed. Nonconflicting items can be raised as areas of shared interest or used as early disclosures to establish a positive negotiating climate. The ratings will give you an idea how to approach your opposer. If conflicting items are extremely important to both sides, you will have to think creatively to achieve your objectives.

Your Objectives	Rating	Conflicts	Opponent's Objectives	Rating	Conflicts

Section IV: Issues/Positions

Issues are specific areas of disagreement. Positions are the views of each side on the issues.

In the following chart:

- List your issues in a form that your opposer will find acceptable
- Add to the list any issues you suspect are important to your opposer or to other major parties but that do not correspond directly to your own issues
- Finally, rate the issues from each side's point of view: 9 = very important; 1= not important

Issue	Rating	
	Yours	Theirs

Now take each issue individually. State your position on the issue. Then write what you feel your opposer's position will be.

Issue: _____

Your position: _____   Opposer's position:

_____   _____

_____   _____

Issue: _____

Your position: _____   Opposer's position:

_____   _____

_____   _____

Issue: _____

Your position: _____   Opposer's position:

_____   _____

_____   _____

Issue: _____

Your position: _____   Opposer's position:

_____   _____

_____   _____

Are there any issues you are willing to concede?

_____

_____

Whom can you contact to determine your opposer's positions on the issues?

_____

_____

Are there any other sources for this information?

_____

_____

Section V: Needs/Gambits

All people are motivated by specific needs. Abraham Maslow identified the common needs that motivate people. Look at the following chart, based upon Maslow's studies, and identify your opposer's needs. Check off those that you feel will motivate him or her in the upcoming negotiation. Remember to consider both the business and the personal needs of your opposer.

Need	Definition	Importance	Will Motivate
Homeostasis	Psychological need for survival-food, warmth, etc.	Most Basic/ Strongest Need	
Safety and security	Safe from emotional or physical harm		
Love and belonging	Friendly association with others		
Esteem	Respect for self and others-status		
Self-actualization	Need to develop and use one's skills		
Knowing and understanding	Seeking knowledge		
Aesthetics	Longing for beauty, aesthetic balance	Least Basic/ Weakest Need	

Now you must decide what specific gambits you will use to move the negotiation in your direction. (Each gambit consists of three elements: need, variety of application, and level of approach.) Remember that the safest tactics are those that work for your cause and satisfy the needs of your opposer.

Write a list of your gambits, then rate them according to how effective you feel they will be: 9 = useful; 1= not useful.

Gambit	Rating

Section VI: Climates

Negotiations involve feelings. The messages you send with your words, actions, and body language set the climate for the talks. Before you enter a negotiation, you should know what climates exits and which ones you want to create.

First, select your negotiating philosophy:

_____ In a successful negotiation, everybody wins

_____ Give a little, get a little

_____ It's survival of the fittest

_____ Negotiation is a game

_____ Act to bring out the best in others

_____ Do unto others as you would have them do unto you

_____ Do unto others, and then beat it

_____ In a successful negotiation, everyone must be bloodied

_____ Good guys finish last

_____ Other: _____

Now think about the possible effects of your philosophy. Would you respond positively to it? Don't be afraid to revise your philosophy if you need to. Remember, the more positive the other side feels about your approach, the more likely it is that your solutions will be both accepted and long-lasting.

If negative climates are checked off in either chart, think of ways you could change them into positive ones. Remember that one of the easiest ways to change a climate is to respond with a climate in direct contrast with it. For example, if your opposer is being closed-minded, you should be open-minded, eager to hear new ideas and develop new methods. This will usually bring your opposer around to the positive climate.

The following chart shows opposite sides of various possible climates. Identify those climates that reflect your current position.

Check off those climates that you would like to create during the negotiation.

	Climate				Climate		
	Current	Feelings	Want To Create		Current	Feelings	Want To Create
Positive				*Negative*			
Supportive				Defensive			
Open-minded				Close-minded			
Reliable				Unreliable			
Ethical				Unprincipled			
Capable				Weak			
Involved				Indifferent			
Sensitive				Insensitive			
Cooperative				Antagonistic			
Reasoning				Unreasoning			
Professional				Amateurish			

Now select the climates that you currently sense from your opposer, then check off those climates you might wish to create to control the climates.

	Climate				Climate		
	Current	Feelings	Want To Create		Current	Feelings	Want To Create
Positive				Negative			
Supportive				Defensive			
Open-minded				Close-minded			
Reliable				Unreliable			
Ethical				Unprincipled			
Capable				Weak			
Involved				Indifferent			
Sensitive				Insensitive			
Cooperative				Antagonistic			
Reasoning				Unreasoning			
Professional				Amateurish			

Section VII: Strategies

On the following pages is a list of strategies, their definitions, and possible countermoves. Strategies fall into three basic categories:

1 When: the timing of the move

2 How and Where: the method and place

3. Other: a combination of method, time, and place

Read through the strategies, paying close attention to those you would want to use for yourself or those that you feel your opposer might use. In choosing the strategies you will use, remember the effect on the climates you are trying to create, your philosophy, and your overall goals, rather than concentrating simply on individual gains.

When Strategies

STRATEGY	DEFINITION	POSSIBLE COUNTERS AND MORE
Forbearance	You delay or avoid taking action. This allows both sides time to reevaluate and make changes.	Forbear in return. Do something unexpected. Leave, or seem to do so. Offer reward if other side agrees to stop forbearing. Focus on specific issues or members of other team.
Surprise	Take an unexpected approach while maintaining your original objective.	Spring surprises in return. Delay in taking action. Take a conservative approach. Cut off the negotiation completely. Caucus, i.e., meet with team members or allies to decide what to do next.
Fait accompli	Pretend a matter is already settled and agreed upon in hopes that the other side will go along.	Get other people involved. Refuse to negotiate further. Bring in new people with new needs. Forbear until assurances are given.
Bland Withdrawal	Leave the room. Stop the negotiation.	Call a recess. Spring surprises in return. Cut off the negotiations. Start at preparation stage again.
Apparent withdrawal	Temporarily withdraw or seem to withdraw, but leave someone behind. Gives the impression of nonchalance and strength.	Same as Bland withdrawal.

STRATEGY	DEFINITION	POSSIBLE COUNTERS AND MORE
Reversal	Do the exact opposite of what opposer expects, or reverse the methods you usually use.	Do the same. Spring some other surprise. Set limits that preclude reversal. Caucus.
Limits	Set a limit—a time limit, a space limit, or a natural limit, e.g., an organizational one.	Make an offer with a self- imposed limit. Bring in a higher authority. Do the opposite; reverse the method. Respond with humor. Make opposer justify the limit.
Feinting	Divert attention by pretending to attack one problem while aiming a blow at another.	Change levels and sidestep the feint. Call in a mediator to discover the real intent. Change the focus of the discussion.

How and Where Strategies

STRATEGY	DEFINITION	POSSIBLE COUNTERS
Participation	Find someone who is also interested in dealing with your problem.	Join forces with someone as well. Try to bring participating party over to other side.
Association	Link certain personal characteristics, attitudes, or actions with those of an influential person or compare the situation to an outstanding event.	Remain unaffected by association. Change level of approach.
Disassociation	Move away from old methods and solutions.	Wait it out. Change level of approach.
Crossroads	Assemble many different strategies and options. Use several at once.	Handle strategies individually. Wait until all strategies are used before acting. Withdraw. Call a mediator.

Successful Selling Made E-Z

STRATEGY	DEFINITION	POSSIBLE COUNTERS
Blanketing	Cover a broad area with your approach in hopes of hitting the target.	Wait it out.
Salami	Slice your objectives into smaller "pieces" to make your proposal easier for the other side to "swallow."	Wait and move at the right time. Let the other side take so much that a counter-reaction is produced. Make the other side's actions very costly.
Bracketing	Deliberately over-shoot, then under-shoot your goal. Helps set limits.	Wait it out. Accept the terms when the other side under-shoots.
Changing levels	Move from level to level, e.g., from a personal to a broader view.	Do something unex-pected. Walk out. Focus on different issues. Set limits that return the negotiation to its previous level.

Other Strategies

STRATEGY	DEFINITION	POSSIBLE COUNTERS
High expectations	Start by making the highest possible demands.	Wait it out. Walk out.
Agent with limited authority	Send someone who has to answer to others for most decisions. Slows talks down.	Find out how and when agent will get approval. Use techni-cal people to raise limits. Try to meet head person alone. Ask how negotiations are expected to be successful with this approach.
Nonnegotiable demands	Present demands as unalterable.	Bring in mediators and arbitrators. Wait it out. Change focus to other issues. Bring in associates to strengthen side.

222

STRATEGY	DEFINITION	POSSIBLE COUNTERS
Good guy/Bad Guy	One person hopeful, the other side hopelessly negative.	Caucus whenever bad guy speaks. Use humor to expose the bad guy. Pretend to take it personally.
Caucus	Meet with team members or allies to decide what to do next.	Limit number of caucuses. Go to caucus each time other side comes out.
Low-balling	Make a ridiculously low offer to drive others out of the market.	Get a commitment on all terms. Be informed as to reasonable terms. Get commitment from the top. Walk away.
Intentional misunderstanding	Bring the other side to agreement by pretending you've made an error. They'll go along with corrections without further discussion.	Refuse to take advantage of the "mistake." Show other advantages. Allow face saving. Bring in a mediator.
Last clear chance	Put the final decision on their side	Wait it out. Get someone else to take the challenge. Bring up another issue. Leave, or appear to leave.
Plateauing	Each time an agreement seems to be reached, up the terms.	Raise the demands. Wait it out. Make surprise demands. Set limits.
Exposure	Let the other side know you're onto them.	Change levels. Wait it out. Bring up new issue.
Face-saving	Avoid certain topics if they would bring shame to you or opposer.	Withdraw. Respect the boundaries. Work around the subject.

STRATEGY	DEFINITION	POSSIBLE COUNTERS
Personalize	Pretend to be personally insulted, even if the other side hasn't done anything to deserve it.	Deny attempt to personalize. Ask forgiveness. Call a caucus.
Sole source supplier	Exercise or threaten to exercise power gained from being the only source available.	Show that price is outside the market limits. Reduce and delay placing orders. Deal with someone else. Show an attempt to eliminate need for the product.

In the following chart, make a list of the strategies you plan to use with your needs gambit and in your negotiations, and write down the counter-moves your opposer might use against them.

Evaluate each strategy you have chosen. Ask yourself:

- How well does this strategy rest with my intuition, feelings, and code of ethics?

- What are the chances it will provoke a negative reaction?

- What is the legality of the strategy? (Find out if you don't know.)

- Will it really resolve the problem constructively?

Strategy	Counter

Be certain each strategy reflects your negotiating philosophy and encourages the climates you wish to create.

Review your gambits and decide which ones fit with your strategies. Plan where you will use them.

Now do the same for your opposer. List possible strategies and counters you would use against them.

Take It a Step Further

Using a computer program to prepare for negotiating offers some important advantages. The interactive nature of the process lets you learn faster and more effectively. You can concentrate on the information you need for the negotiation itself, and you do not need to be concerned with creating or working within a structure for laying out your plan.

The computer works with you and keeps you focused, moving forward in the direction you want to go, and keeping track of important information so that no detail is overlooked. You can be as candid as you like, because the computer will not judge your opinions or your level of skill. There's no need to worry about sharing your ideas or comments with an unappreciative audience. All important details of the preparation will be processed and can be printed out for you and your team to use for practice and for reference during the negotiating session. Later on, you can use part or all of your plan to guide you in other situations. You've got an automated negotiating "coach" to work with whenever you need help.

For Building Your Problem Solving Skills

The Art of Negotiating® Software makes negotiation preparation an interactive, automated process that uses the power of your computer to make you a more effective negotiator. In the same way, The Idea Generator® Plus, based on another work of Gerard I. Nierenberg, *The Art of Creative Thinking*, helps you come up with a list of workable ideas.

You'll state your problem in clear, concise terms and use seven proved techniques to increase your problem-solving effectiveness. You'll see the problem, or the challenge, from fresh perspectives, try on other people's points of view, and learn new approaches that can lead to breakthrough thinking. Using your computer's capability, you'll get to "Aha!" faster than you possibly could on your own.

Glossary of Useful Terms

A-C◆◆◆◆

Aesthetic needs

The need for order, balance, and beauty.

Agenda

A list of issues in the order in which they will be discussed during the negotiation.

Assumption

The basis of any "fact," whether true or false, that you or your opposer takes for granted. Assumptions must be questioned to verify if they can be used as actual facts. If not, they should be abandoned before the negotiation begins.

Brainstorming

A technique developed more than 50 years ago that stimulates the random expression of ideas by a group of individuals. The theory behind brainstorming is that the airing of problems and ideas generates new ideas. Every idea that comes from a brainstorming session should be transcribed and reviewed. The validity of each concept or idea can then be determined later, after a careful evaluation of the transcript.

Climate

The feeling surrounding a negotiation: trusting or suspicious, supportive or defensive. You try to change negative climates into positive ones, so that the negotiation does not become an emotional contest and the parties feel that they each can win something.

Conceptual knowledge

Ideas that cannot be verified by the senses.

Concessions

Any point in a negotiation that you are willing to concede to the opposer. One gives a concession on one point in hopes of getting one on another.

E-H✦✦✦

Esteem needs

Every person's need for self-respect, a feeling of personal worth, adequacy, and competence.

Extensional world

The physical world that exists outside the mind.

Fact

Information that is known: (1) because it conforms to reality and can be verified, (2) because it is a teaching we believe in, (3) because we feel that way, and (4) because it is valid according to the rules of a system.

Gambits

Specific actions you can take to move a negotiation toward resolution. Each gambit has three elements—need, variety of application, and level of approach.

General semantics

The study of the relationship between symbols (especially language) and reality. Understanding how people relate language to the world around them helps us understand the adjustments they make in response to each other and the environment.

Group drama

Also known as psychodrama or sociodrama. Participants play roles of opposing sides or forces to foresee and experience possible reactions that might occur during an upcoming negotiation.

Hierarchy of needs

Human needs fall into the following categories, with number one being the most basic need and number seven the least: (1) homeostatic needs, (2) safety and security needs, (3) love and belonging needs, (4) esteem needs, (5) self-actualization needs, (6) knowing and understanding needs, and (7) aesthetic needs.

Homeostatic needs

Physiological needs, including the need for food, warmth, shelter, water, sleep, and sexual fulfillment.

I-O◆◆◆◆

Intentional world

The world that exists within our minds.

Issues

Specific areas of disagreement to be discussed during a negotiation.

Knowing and understanding needs

The need to know about our environment, to explore, and to understand our lives.

Levels of negotiation

Interpersonal (between individuals); Interorganizational (between organizations); International (between nations).

Love and belonging needs

The need to feel a part of a group, to belong to and be with someone else.

Meta-talk

The hidden implications in what you say that can change the meaning. It is a mask we hide behind.

Need theory of negotiation

Working for our own and our opposer's needs to get a desired result in a negotiation. The theory allows us to use alternative methods to work with, counteract, or modify an opposer's actions, which are dictated by his or her needs.

Negotiation

The exchange of ideas for the purpose of changing a relationship.

Nonverbal communications

Gestures and expressions that communicate feelings without the use of words. Sometimes known as "body language."

Objectives

The desired results of the negotiation.

P-T◆◆◆

Perceptual knowledge

Knowledge derived from things that can be touched or perceived directly.

Positions

Each side's view on the issues that will be discussed during a negotiation.

Safety and security needs

The need to feel safe from injury, both physical and emotional.

Self-actualization

The need to become what one is capable of being.

Strategies

The means of implementing negotiating gambits. Strategies are the long-range plan of the negotiating process from conception to completion.

Subject

What your negotiation is about. It is important that both sides agree on the subject of the negotiation.

Tactics

Devices used to implement the strategies used in the actual process of negotiation.

Index